The Love That Remains

The Love That Remains

A YEAR OF HEALING AFTER LOSS

A Daily Companion for Connecting
with Spirit from a Psychic Medium

ALYSSA MALEHORN

The Love That Remains:
A Year of Healing After Loss
A Daily Companion for Connecting with Spirit from a Psychic
Medium

Copyright © 2026 Alyssa Malehorn

This book is intended for inspirational and personal use only. It is not a substitute for professional medical, psychological, or spiritual advice. The author does not diagnose, treat, or prescribe.

Interior design by: C. Warren
Printed in the United States of America
First Edition

ISBN: 979-8-9948473-0-5

Published by Raw Spirituality LLC
www.alyssamalehorn.com

To Zack — my beloved partner in all things — thank you for walking this path of remembrance and embodiment beside me, with your love, humor, and infinite soul strength.

To my son, Wolf, who reminds me every day that love is a living, curious, and ever-expanding energy — you are my heart.

And to my cherished ones in Spirit — my sweet Daddy, my soul sister Angie, deeply loved family and friends, and all those who have gone before — your presence is the ground beneath this offering.

This book is for you, and for every heart learning how to carry love beyond form.

Contents

Author's Note

G rief is not a problem to be solved — it is a sacred
   passage to be honored. If you're holding this
book, it likely means someone you love is no longer here
in the way they once were. Your heart is learning how to
live inside that absence. I want you to know: you're not
alone.

As a psychic medium, I've spent a lifetime listening
to the voices of the departed — and many sacred years
walking beside those who remain. Spirit reminds us,
again and again, that love does not end with death. It
reshapes. It reaches across dimensions. It becomes the
bridge between worlds.

This book was born from thousands of soul
conversations — with clients, students, and the departed
alike. It is an offering for that bridge. It's for the ones
who are grieving but still loving. Hurting and trying to
stay open. You don't need any special gifts to feel the

presence of your loved one. You only need a willing heart, a quiet moment, and the courage to keep showing up.

The Love That Remains is a daily companion to walk with you through the landscape of grief. Each day offers a gentle prompt and a message from Spirit—to help you feel supported, seen, and connected to your own inner wisdom and the unseen love that surrounds you.

There is no right way to grieve. There is only your way. This book is not a map—it's a lantern. May it light the path ahead, one day at a time.

May your grief become sacred ground.

May your connection endure in new and surprising ways.

And may the love that remains carry you forward, one breath at a time.

With you in love,

Alyssa

How to Use This Book

G rief does not follow a straight line, and healing
rarely happens all at once. This book is not meant
to rush your process, but to gently accompany you as
you move through it—day by day, breath by breath.

Each page offers:

+ *A daily prompt*—to help you reflect on your
emotions, memories, and inner experience.

+ *A spirit insight*—a message brought through from
the loving, unseen world to remind you that you are not
alone.

You may choose to begin at the start of a calendar
month, on the day your loss occurred, or simply turn
to the page that calls to you. There is no wrong way to
journey through this book.

There is room to write on each page if you feel called
to journal your thoughts. Let this be a sacred space: a
place to honor your loved one, your healing, and the
invisible threads of connection that remain.

If a certain day feels too tender, skip it and return
later. If one reflection brings you comfort, revisit it as
often as you need. Your intuition will guide you.

Above all, let this be an offering of love—for the one
you lost, for the spirit that remains, and for your own
heart as it heals.

MONTH ONE

The First Light:
Grounding in Grief

I n the earliest days of grief, the world can feel
unrecognizable. You may feel numb, disoriented,
or overwhelmed by a sadness that seems impossible to
hold.

This month is not about fixing anything—it's about
allowing. Allowing yourself to feel what you feel. To be
where you are. To move slowly. You don't need to be
strong right now. You just need to be.

I'll be here with you, every step—holding this space
with compassion, reminding you that your pain is not a
problem. It's proof of your love. And even now, in the
quiet, your loved one is near.

DAY 1

What does grief feel like in your body today?

Your body remembers. It holds your grief as gently as it can. Let it speak. Notice the sensations without trying to change them. They are not here to punish you. They are here to express the depth of what matters. This awareness is an act of presence—and presence is healing.

_____

_____

_____

_____

_____

_____

_____

_____

_____

_____

_____

_____

_____

DAY 2

I miss you most when...

You know the moments — quiet ones, unexpected ones, milestones you thought you'd share. That ache you feel? It's not emptiness. It's where your love still lives. When longing rises, Spirit often draws close. Missing them is not a step backward. It's your heart whispering, "I remember."

_____

_____

_____

_____

_____

_____

_____

_____

_____

_____

_____

_____

_____

_____

DAY 3

If I could tell you one thing right now,
it would be...

S peak it aloud or write it down. They hear you. You are not speaking into silence. Let your words be a bridge between worlds. Connection doesn't end at death. It just changes shape.

_____

_____

_____

_____

_____

_____

_____

_____

_____

_____

_____

_____

_____

DAY 4

A memory that brings both tears and love is...

L et yourself feel both at once. That mixture of sorrow
 and sweetness is sacred. It means the love was real.
It still is.

_____
_____
_____
_____
_____
_____
_____
_____
_____
_____
_____
_____
_____
_____
_____
_____
_____
_____

DAY 5

Describe where you were when you first heard the news of their passing.

E ven if it's painful, your story matters. Telling it helps integrate the shock. You don't have to relive it all—just offer it a place to land.

_____

_____

_____

_____

_____

_____

_____

_____

_____

_____

_____

_____

_____

_____

_____

_____

DAY 6

What has surprised me most about grief is...

G rief doesn't always look how we imagined. It reshapes us in ways we never expect. Let the surprises come without judgment. You are allowed to change.

_____
_____
_____
_____
_____
_____
_____
_____
_____
_____
_____
_____
_____
_____
_____
_____
_____
_____

DAY 7

Today, I give myself permission to feel...

There are no wrong emotions. Only signals from the heart. Whatever arises belongs. Your truth is welcome here.

_____
_____
_____
_____
_____
_____
_____
_____
_____
_____
_____
_____
_____
_____
_____
_____
_____
_____

DAY 8

Write a letter to your grief as if it were a companion. What would you say to it?

S ometimes grief feels like a shadow walking beside us. Other times, it lives inside. Either way, it softens when acknowledged. Even shadows long to be understood.

_____

_____

_____

_____

_____

_____

_____

_____

_____

_____

_____

_____

_____

_____

_____

_____

DAY 9

My heart is heavy with...

L et the weight be spoken. You don't have to carry it all in silence. This heaviness is not weakness. It is devotion.

_____

_____

_____

_____

_____

_____

_____

_____

_____

_____

_____

_____

_____

_____

_____

_____

DAY 10

*What part of my daily life has changed
the most since their passing?*

L oss lives in routines. In the empty chair, the
unopened message, the unspoken thought. Grieve
the small things. They mattered, too.

_____

_____

_____

_____

_____

_____

_____

_____

_____

_____

_____

_____

_____

_____

_____

_____

DAY 11

What do I need more of right now?
(Rest, space, nourishment, comfort?)

A sk. Let yourself receive. Your needs are not burdens — they are invitations. To be human is to need. To allow those needs is sacred.

_____
_____
_____
_____
_____
_____
_____
_____
_____
_____
_____
_____
_____
_____
_____
_____
_____
_____

DAY 12

One thing thing I wish others understood about my grief is...

Y ou don't owe anyone an explanation. But your truth still matters. Let this be a place where your experience is named and honored.

_____

_____

_____

_____

_____

_____

_____

_____

_____

_____

_____

_____

_____

_____

_____

_____

_____

DAY 13

A ritual that brings me comfort is...

I t doesn't have to be elaborate. Light a candle. Whisper
their name. Breathe. Comfort can live in the smallest
sacred acts.

DAY 14

How has my relationship with time changed since the loss?

G rief rewrites the calendar. Time may stretch, collapse, or spiral. You are not behind. You are moving with your own sacred rhythm.

_____
_____
_____
_____
_____
_____
_____
_____
_____
_____
_____
_____
_____
_____
_____
_____

DAY 15

If my grief could speak, it would say...

W hat words rise up? Don't censor them. Let grief speak in its own language. It may carry a message from the soul.

_____
_____
_____
_____
_____
_____
_____
_____
_____
_____
_____
_____
_____
_____
_____
_____
_____

DAY 16

What is one gentle thing I can do for myself today?

E ven a breath counts. A pause. A kind word.
Gentleness is a medicine the soul understands.

_____
_____
_____
_____
_____
_____
_____
_____
_____
_____
_____
_____
_____
_____
_____
_____
_____
_____

DAY 17

A memory I want to hold onto forever is...

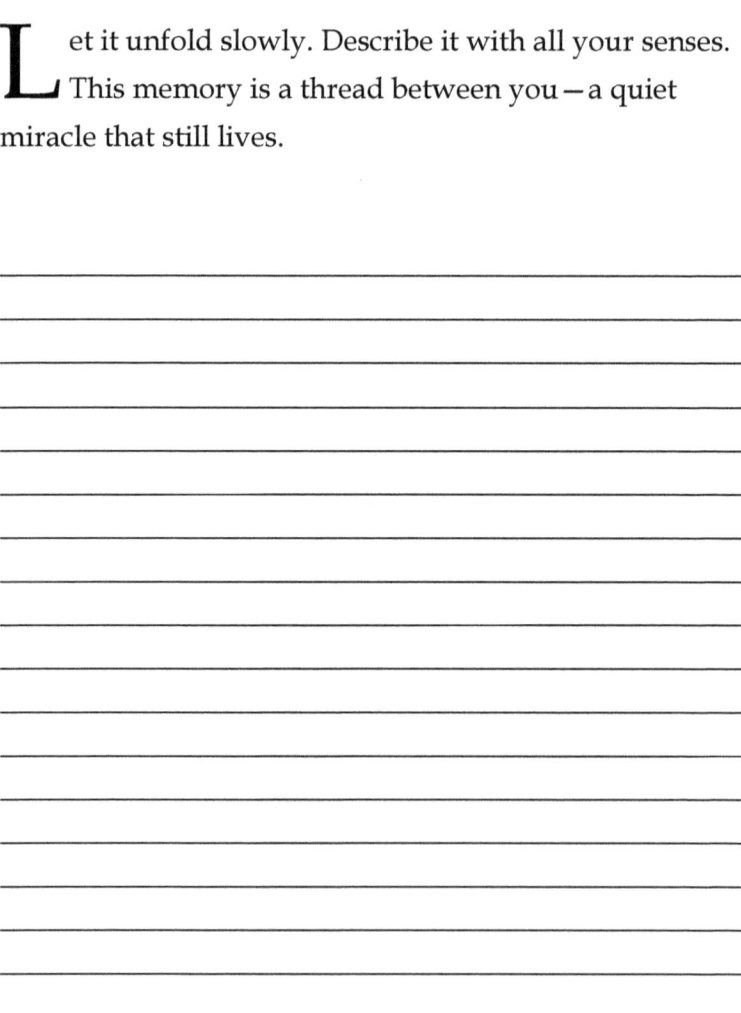

L et it unfold slowly. Describe it with all your senses. This memory is a thread between you — a quiet miracle that still lives.

_____
_____
_____
_____
_____
_____
_____
_____
_____
_____
_____
_____
_____
_____
_____
_____
_____
_____

DAY 18

What emotion is beneath the surface today that I haven't acknowledged?

Grief can layer itself in quiet ways. What's waiting beneath? All of you belongs here. Nothing is too much.

_____
_____
_____
_____
_____
_____
_____
_____
_____
_____
_____
_____
_____
_____
_____
_____
_____
_____

DAY 19

When I look at photos of them, I feel...

L et the feeling arrive without defense. Their image is not the past. It's a portal to presence.

_____
_____
_____
_____
_____
_____
_____
_____
_____
_____
_____
_____
_____
_____
_____
_____
_____
_____
_____
_____
_____

DAY 20

If I could sit beside them one more time,
I would...

L et yourself imagine it. Don't rush. This longing is a
form of prayer.

DAY 21

I feel most grounded when I...

G rief can unroot you. This is your way back to steadiness. Find what holds you — even if only for a moment.

_____

_____

_____

_____

_____

_____

_____

_____

_____

_____

_____

_____

_____

_____

_____

_____

_____

DAY 22

My grief today feels like: (choose a metaphor—weather, animal, color, etc.)

L et your imagination speak. Metaphor is the soul's shorthand. What you choose reveals your inner knowing.

_____

_____

_____

_____

_____

_____

_____

_____

_____

_____

_____

_____

_____

_____

_____

_____

_____

DAY 23

What has grief revealed to me about love?

✦

Y ou're discovering that love doesn't disappear. It transforms. This depth of pain means your love was deep, too.

_____
_____
_____
_____
_____
_____
_____
_____
_____
_____
_____
_____
_____
_____
_____
_____
_____
_____

DAY 24

A song, smell, or place that instantly brings them back to me is...

T hese echoes are not coincidences. They may be soul signals. Receive them as visits.

_____
_____
_____
_____
_____
_____
_____
_____
_____
_____
_____
_____
_____
_____
_____
_____
_____
_____
_____

DAY 25

What is something I need to release today?

R eleasing is not rejection. It's honoring what no longer needs to be held. Let it rise. Let it speak. Let it go.

_____

_____

_____

_____

_____

_____

_____

_____

_____

_____

_____

_____

_____

_____

_____

_____

_____

DAY 26

In what ways am I honoring their memory, even in small moments?

Y ou may not realize how much you're doing, but Spirit does. Every act of remembrance is a continuation of love.

_____
_____
_____
_____
_____
_____
_____
_____
_____
_____
_____
_____
_____
_____
_____
_____
_____
_____

DAY 27

How do I speak to myself when I'm hurting? What do I need to hear instead?

Your inner voice can become a sanctuary. Let it be soft. Speak to yourself with gentleness, with love.

DAY 28

My grief is teaching me...

G rief is a teacher cloaked in pain, but its wisdom is real. Let the lesson come in its own time.

DAY 29

What do I want to remember about this part of the journey?

Y ou are surviving what once felt unsurvivable. This chapter is not a detour. It's a holy part of your life.

_____
_____
_____
_____
_____
_____
_____
_____
_____
_____
_____
_____
_____
_____
_____
_____

DAY 30

Write a message of comfort to your future self—what would you want to hear on a hard day?

This is your love letter forward in time. Remind yourself that healing is happening, even when it feels far away.

_____
_____
_____
_____
_____
_____
_____
_____
_____
_____
_____
_____
_____

MONTH TWO

Healing the Unsaid

There's often so much left unspoken when someone we love passes. Regrets. What-ifs. The words we didn't get to say — or the ones we wish we could take back.

This month is a space for healing the unfinished business of the heart. And here's the beautiful truth: Spirit knows. They hear you now. They understand more deeply on the other side than they ever could here.

I'll be right here with you, helping you give voice to what's been held in silence. As a medium, I've seen time and time again — healing doesn't end with death. It just begins in a new way.

DAY 1

What words did you never get the chance to say? Write them now.

Spirit hears you clearly, even now. You are never too late to speak love or truth. Say the words. This space is safe and sacred. Nothing is too small or too late when it comes from the heart.

_____

_____

_____

_____

_____

_____

_____

_____

_____

_____

_____

_____

_____

_____

_____

DAY 2

Was there conflict, confusion, or tension at the time of their passing? What do you wish had been different?

S pirit sees the whole picture now. Compassion flows easily on the other side. You can bring peace to places where pain once lived. Let the light in.

_____
_____
_____
_____
_____
_____
_____
_____
_____
_____
_____
_____
_____
_____
_____
_____
_____
_____

DAY 3

Write a letter beginning with: "I forgive you for..." and allow yourself to release.

Forgiveness is a balm for both souls. Every word you write is a thread in your freedom. Let your heart speak honestly. You don't need to carry this alone.

_____
_____
_____
_____
_____
_____
_____
_____
_____
_____
_____
_____
_____
_____
_____
_____

DAY 4

Now write: "I forgive myself for..."
and speak gently to your heart.

Self-forgiveness is not forgetting — it's remembering your humanity. Spirit holds no judgment. Offer yourself the grace you so easily give to others.

_____

_____

_____

_____

_____

_____

_____

_____

_____

_____

_____

_____

_____

_____

_____

_____

_____

_____

DAY 5

What is one thing you wish you could have done differently? Speak it aloud.

Your loved one isn't holding blame—only love. Let that truth soften the edges of regret. You are worthy of peace.

_____
_____
_____
_____
_____
_____
_____
_____
_____
_____
_____
_____
_____
_____
_____
_____

DAY 6

What emotions have you been afraid to feel? Can you give them space today?

Avoiding the feeling doesn't erase it. Let it rise gently. You are safe. Spirit surrounds you with tenderness.

_____

_____

_____

_____

_____

_____

_____

_____

_____

_____

_____

_____

_____

_____

_____

_____

_____

DAY 7

*Have you been holding guilt? What can
you imagine they would they say to that?*

In Spirit, they want only your peace. Guilt is heavy;
love is light. Their message is simple: You did
enough.

_____

_____

_____

_____

_____

_____

_____

_____

_____

_____

_____

_____

_____

_____

_____

_____

DAY 8

What do you believe they already knew,
even if you didn't say it?

S o often the unsaid was already known. Spirit felt the love beneath your silence. That knowing still connects your hearts.

_____
_____
_____
_____
_____
_____
_____
_____
_____
_____
_____
_____
_____
_____
_____

DAY 9

If you could rewrite one moment in your relationship, what would it be? What would you say now?

Healing moves both ways. Picture the moment anew. You are not bound by time when it comes to love.

_____

_____

_____

_____

_____

_____

_____

_____

_____

_____

_____

_____

_____

_____

DAY 10

Are you afraid they didn't know how much you loved them? What proof did you give, even without words?

Love is not always loud. It shows up in presence, care, and sometimes even 'tough love'. Spirit saw all of it. You loved well.

_____

_____

_____

_____

_____

_____

_____

_____

_____

_____

_____

_____

_____

_____

_____

_____

DAY 11

Have you experienced shame or regret
about how they passed?
What needs to be spoken?

Here is no punishment, only perspective. Let shame dissolve in the light of truth. You are not alone. Spirit walks beside you.

_____
_____
_____
_____
_____
_____
_____
_____
_____
_____
_____
_____
_____
_____
_____
_____

DAY 12

Imagine sitting face to face with them.
What would you say?
What would they say back?

L et your imagination open the door. Conversations
continue across the veil. Feel their love as it reaches
you now.

_____

_____

_____

_____

_____

_____

_____

_____

_____

_____

_____

_____

_____

_____

_____

DAY 13

Write a letter of apology—even if it's to yourself. What needs to be released?

This is about release, not blame. Spirit supports every step of your healing. You are allowed to begin again.

_____
_____
_____
_____
_____
_____
_____
_____
_____
_____
_____
_____
_____
_____
_____
_____

DAY 14

What do you wish had been different in your relationship overall? Let it be seen.

Y ou don't have to pretend it was perfect. Love makes room for the whole truth. Spirit honors the complexity with grace.

_____
_____
_____
_____
_____
_____
_____
_____
_____
_____
_____
_____
_____
_____
_____
_____
_____
_____

DAY 15

If you had more time with them, what would you do differently? What did you do beautifully?

We focus on what we missed, but Spirit sees what was given. Let their view become your own: You gave perfectly.

_____
_____
_____
_____
_____
_____
_____
_____
_____
_____
_____
_____
_____
_____
_____
_____

DAY 16

Do you carry a story of "not enough"?
What would it feel like to rewrite
that today?

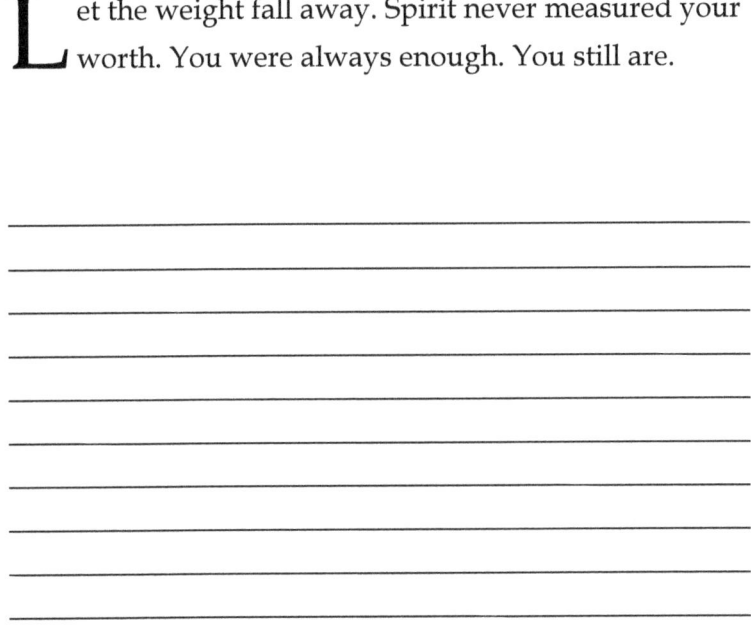

L et the weight fall away. Spirit never measured your
worth. You were always enough. You still are.

_____
_____
_____
_____
_____
_____
_____
_____
_____
_____
_____
_____
_____
_____
_____
_____

DAY 17

What are you afraid others won't understand about your grief or your relationship? Say it here.

This is your truth. You don't need outside validation to know what was real. Spirit understands. I understand.

DAY 18

*Write a blessing of peace for your past
self. They carried a lot.*

Your past self deserves tenderness, not criticism. Let
this blessing wrap around you both.

_____

_____

_____

_____

_____

_____

_____

_____

_____

_____

_____

_____

_____

_____

_____

_____

DAY 19

If you've felt judged by others for how you're grieving, write what you wish they understood.

G rief has no timeline. Your path is sacred. Spirit
walks with you, not with their opinions.

_____
_____
_____
_____
_____
_____
_____
_____
_____
_____
_____
_____
_____
_____

DAY 20

Did you have a complicated relationship?
Name both the beauty and the pain.

✦

Complication doesn't cancel love. Spirit now sees the
whole picture — and holds it all with compassion.

_____
_____
_____
_____
_____
_____
_____
_____
_____
_____
_____
_____
_____
_____
_____
_____
_____

DAY 21

If they passed suddenly, what did you want more time for?

I t's okay to name the longing. The story isn't over. Spirit still receives your heart.

DAY 22

Do you fear they're disappointed in you?
What might their higher self say instead?

S pirit speaks only in love. Let that voice be louder than fear. You are not judged. You are cherished.

_____
_____
_____
_____
_____
_____
_____
_____
_____
_____
_____
_____
_____
_____
_____
_____

DAY 23

*What do you believe their soul is asking
you to release today?*

L et an exhale of the pain go. Keep the love. You are
not letting them go — you are freeing both of you.

_____

_____

_____

_____

_____

_____

_____

_____

_____

_____

_____

_____

_____

_____

_____

DAY 24

Create a ritual of release: light a candle, speak the unsaid, and let the flame carry it upward.

S pirit meets you in sacred moments. Your words are received, always.

_____
_____
_____
_____
_____
_____
_____
_____
_____
_____
_____
_____
_____
_____
_____
_____

DAY 25

Have you blamed yourself for something beyond your control? Speak it now. Then breathe.

Y ou are not responsible for everything. Let Spirit hold what you cannot. Forgiveness is already flowing toward you.

_____
_____
_____
_____
_____
_____
_____
_____
_____
_____
_____
_____
_____
_____
_____

DAY 26

*What would it feel like to be completely
understood by them right now?
Let that feeling in.*

T hey understand. Let yourself be seen through the
eyes of love. You are safe in their knowing.

_____
_____
_____
_____
_____
_____
_____
_____
_____
_____
_____
_____
_____
_____
_____
_____

DAY 27

Write a new story about your relationship—not one defined by pain, but by growth.

T his story still matters. Let it be shaped by love, healing, and the beauty of becoming.

_____
_____
_____
_____
_____
_____
_____
_____
_____
_____
_____
_____
_____
_____
_____
_____
_____
_____

DAY 28

What do you want to carry forward from your connection with them?

L ove is not lost. It becomes a part of who you are. Let their presence live on through your kindness, your courage, your light.

_____

_____

_____

_____

_____

_____

_____

_____

_____

_____

_____

_____

_____

_____

DAY 29

What part of your heart still needs reassurance? What would you want them to say to that part?

I magine their voice, gentle and true. Let their love become the answer your heart has been waiting for.

_____

_____

_____

_____

_____

_____

_____

_____

_____

_____

_____

_____

_____

_____

_____

DAY 30

Write a message of closure or continuation—whatever feels most honest.

C losure isn't the end. It's a turning point. Or maybe it's not closure you need, but a new way to stay connected. Let your words seal this chapter with grace and presence. Spirit is listening.

_____

_____

_____

_____

_____

_____

_____

_____

_____

_____

_____

_____

_____

_____

_____

_____

MONTH THREE

Inviting Spirit:
The Veil is Thin

Though their body is gone, their essence remains. You might feel it already — in a dream, a whisper, a shiver down your spine, or a feather on your path.

This month is about opening gently to those subtle moments. You don't need to be a medium to connect with Spirit — you just need love and a willingness to listen. As someone who walks between worlds, I'm here to remind you: the veil is thin. Your loved one is still with you. And even if you doubt what you feel at first, I'm here to help you trust your own sacred knowing.

DAY 1

*Think back to a time you felt your loved
one near. What happened? How did it feel?*

T hat moment was real. Spirit often connects when
you least expect it — your heart knows the truth
before your mind does. Let that memory become a
confirmation, not a question.

_____

_____

_____

_____

_____

_____

_____

_____

_____

_____

_____

_____

_____

_____

DAY 2

If your loved one were standing beside you today, what would they want you to know?

S pirit often says, "I'm okay. I love you. I haven't left." These messages come softly, but clearly. Feel their love echo through your heart, again and again.

_____
_____
_____
_____
_____
_____
_____
_____
_____
_____
_____
_____
_____
_____
_____

DAY 3

Describe your loved one's energy—not just their personality, but how it felt to be around them.

Their essence is how they still visit you. That feeling is the signature of their soul. Their energy still surrounds you—it always has.

_____

_____

_____

_____

_____

_____

_____

_____

_____

_____

_____

_____

_____

_____

_____

DAY 4

*Set the intention:
"I invite your presence today." What
unfolds when you say this out loud?*

Intentions are like beacons of light. You don't have to
know how to connect—you just have to be willing.
Spirit responds to sincerity, not perfection.

DAY 5

What signs or synchronicities have you noticed lately that might be from Spirit?

S pirit communicates through patterns, symbols, and resonance. If something made you stop and feel — trust it. Emotion is often the echo of their touch.

_____

_____

_____

_____

_____

_____

_____

_____

_____

_____

_____

_____

_____

_____

_____

_____

DAY 6

*Choose a number, word, or symbol that
represents your loved one.
Watch for it today.*

T his becomes a shared language between you. It
doesn't need to be logical — it just needs to feel true.
You are creating a bridge across dimensions.

_____

_____

_____

_____

_____

_____

_____

_____

_____

_____

_____

_____

_____

DAY 7

What time of day do you most feel their
presence? What might that mean?

S pirit often draws near when the world is quiet—
dawn, dusk, midnight. Notice your rhythms. They
may be moving in step with you.

_____

_____

_____

_____

_____

_____

_____

_____

_____

_____

_____

_____

_____

_____

_____

_____

DAY 8

If they could send you a song right now,
what do you imagine it would be?

Songs often carry messages wrapped in melody. Let the lyrics speak to you as if whispered from Spirit.

_____
_____
_____
_____
_____
_____
_____
_____
_____
_____
_____
_____
_____
_____
_____
_____
_____

DAY 9

*Write a dialogue between you and your
loved one. Don't filter, just let it flow.*

This is one of the most powerful tools I know. You
are not imagining. You are remembering. Love
writes through your pen.

_____

_____

_____

_____

_____

_____

_____

_____

_____

_____

_____

_____

_____

_____

_____

_____

_____

DAY 10

Light a candle and speak to them.
What comes through in the stillness?

✦

Candles create space. Stillness opens the door. Even if you hear nothing, trust what you feel.

_____
_____
_____
_____
_____
_____
_____
_____
_____
_____
_____
_____
_____
_____
_____
_____
_____

DAY 11

Have you ever felt tingles, warmth, or a gentle pressure? Spirit often speaks through sensation.

S pirit communicates in touchless touch. A breeze, a felt awareness, a sense of someone near. Your body knows before your mind does.

_____
_____
_____
_____
_____
_____
_____
_____
_____
_____
_____
_____
_____
_____

DAY 12

Ask your loved one to visit you in a dream, if it's possible for them. What would you like to ask or feel in that dream?

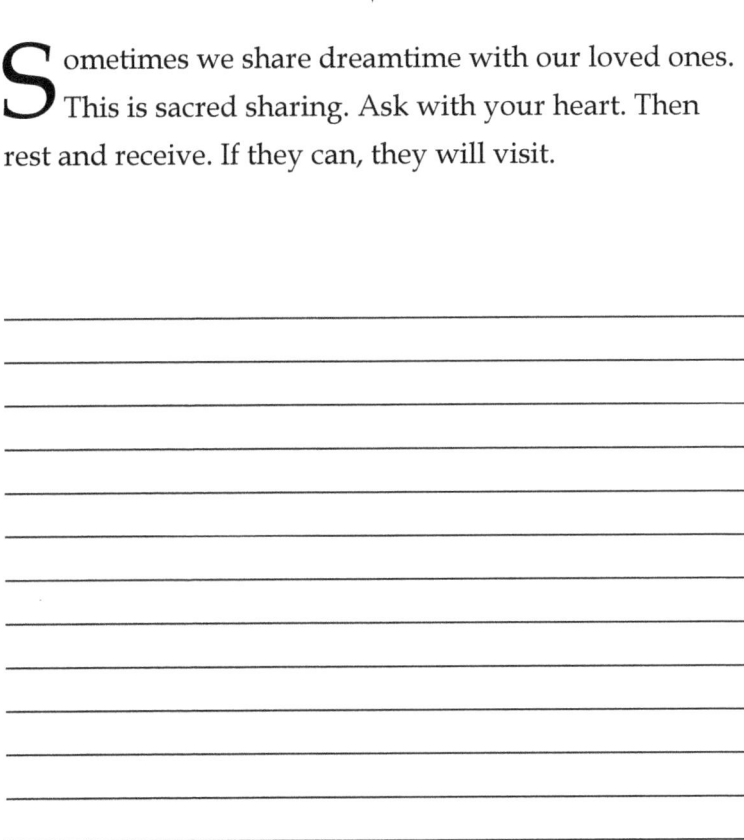

Sometimes we share dreamtime with our loved ones. This is sacred sharing. Ask with your heart. Then rest and receive. If they can, they will visit.

_____

_____

_____

_____

_____

_____

_____

_____

_____

_____

_____

_____

_____

_____

DAY 13

Think of a scent that reminds you of them. Can you recall it now? Invite it in.

C lairolfaction (psychic scent) is real. Memory alone doesn't carry scent—Spirit does. Let the aroma be a soft reunion.

DAY 14

Look at a photo of them today, if you have one. Envision them in your mind, if you don't. What do their eyes say to you?

Photos hold energetic memory. Their gaze may still speak to you. Look with your heart — not just your eyes.

_____
_____
_____
_____
_____
_____
_____
_____
_____
_____
_____
_____
_____
_____
_____

DAY 15

Sit in silence for three minutes and place your hand on your heart. Invite their energy to join you.

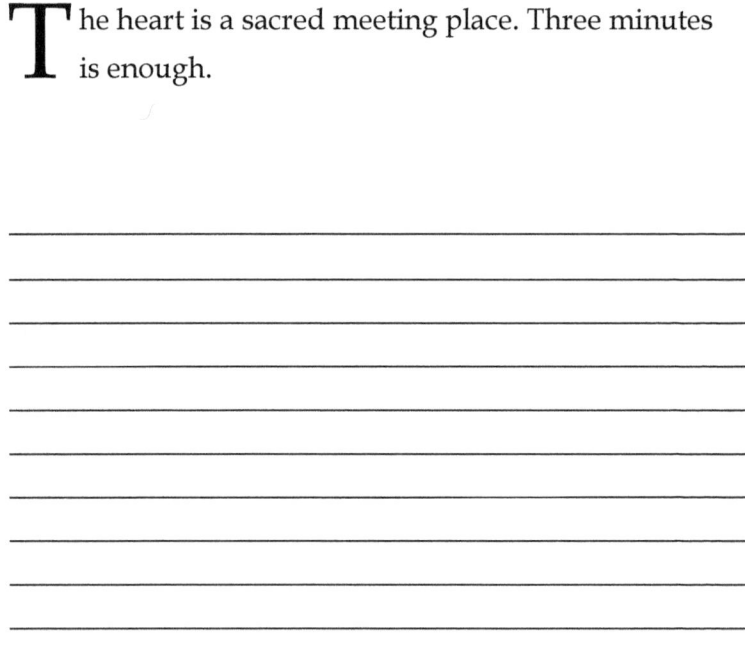

T he heart is a sacred meeting place. Three minutes is enough.

DAY 16

Today, write a message from them to you.
Let their love speak through your pen.

✦

S pirit will use your words to comfort your soul.
Don't edit. Don't doubt. Let it flow.

_____

_____

_____

_____

_____

_____

_____

_____

_____

_____

_____

_____

_____

_____

_____

_____

_____

DAY 17

What would it feel like to truly believe they are with you? Try living that truth for one day.

I magine walking through your day with their love beside you. See what shifts. Belief makes space for magic.

_____
_____
_____
_____
_____
_____
_____
_____
_____
_____
_____
_____
_____
_____
_____
_____

DAY 18

Create a small altar or sacred space for connection. What items will you include?

Photos, stones, feathers, candles — anything infused with memory and meaning. This space becomes a lighthouse where their presence can meet you.

_____

_____

_____

_____

_____

_____

_____

_____

_____

_____

_____

_____

_____

_____

_____

_____

_____

DAY 19

Do you feel your intuition is shifting since their passing? How has your inner world changed?

L oss can break something open. Often, what comes through that break is light. Your senses are expanding to meet them.

_____
_____
_____
_____
_____
_____
_____
_____
_____
_____
_____
_____
_____
_____

DAY 20

Ask Spirit: "Show me something today that reminds me of our unbreakable bond."

Then let go. Stay open. Spirit will surprise you. It might be subtle—but it will be real.

_____
_____
_____
_____
_____
_____
_____
_____
_____
_____
_____
_____
_____
_____

DAY 21

Recall a moment of comfort since their
passing. What do you believe it meant?

✦

Comfort is often Spirit's way of saying, "Yes, I'm here." Don't brush it away. Let it stay.

_____
_____
_____
_____
_____
_____
_____
_____
_____
_____
_____
_____
_____
_____
_____

DAY 22

Speak their name with love today.
Feel their response.

N ames carry energy. Saying their name is like
knocking on a familiar door. Spirit often answers
through the heart.

DAY 23

What are your senses telling you today? Spirit often communicates through subtle knowing.

The feeling in your chest. The quiet pull to open up. The inner "yes." These are Spirit's gentle nudges.

_____

_____

_____

_____

_____

_____

_____

_____

_____

_____

_____

_____

_____

_____

_____

_____

DAY 24

Write a stream-of-consciousness letter
beginning with: "I feel you when..."

L et the words arrive unfiltered. Don't try to be
poetic — just be true. Spirit writes between the lines.

_____
_____
_____
_____
_____
_____
_____
_____
_____
_____
_____
_____
_____
_____
_____
_____
_____
_____
_____

DAY 25

Have you heard their voice in your mind or heart? What did they say?

Y ou're not imagining it. Spirit often uses the inner voice to comfort and guide. That voice of love is real.

_____

_____

_____

_____

_____

_____

_____

_____

_____

_____

_____

_____

_____

_____

DAY 26

Take a photo or video in nature today.
Look again—what small wonder might be
a hello from Spirit?

A sparkle of light, a shift in the trees, a winged messenger. Spirit speaks through beauty. Nature listens with you.

_____
_____
_____
_____
_____
_____
_____
_____
_____
_____
_____
_____
_____
_____
_____
_____
_____

DAY 27

*Let a moment of stillness today become a
doorway. What do you sense?*

S tillness is not emptiness — it is presence. Breathe.
Feel. Spirit is near.

DAY 28

Imagine your loved one placing a gentle hand on your shoulder. What do you feel in that gesture?

T hat warmth, that pressure, that memory—it's not just imagination. It's an imprint of their love, still reaching.

_____
_____
_____
_____
_____
_____
_____
_____
_____
_____
_____
_____
_____
_____

DAY 29

What message of hope do you feel them sending you today?

Hope may arrive in whispers. In symbols. In songs. Let yourself believe.

_____

_____

_____

_____

_____

_____

_____

_____

_____

_____

_____

_____

_____

_____

_____

_____

DAY 30

Write a thank you letter to your loved one for continuing the connection.

Gratitude opens the veil even more. This connection is real, living, sacred — and it continues.

MONTH FOUR

Conversations Beyond the Veil

Y ou don't need to be a trained psychic to speak with
Spirit. Your heart is already the telephone line —
and love is the signal that makes it ring.

This month, we explore gentle, soul-led ways to
communicate with your loved one on the other side.
Whether through journaling, meditation, dreams, signs,
or simple presence, these prompts will help you practice
tuning in.

I'll be beside you every step of the way, reminding you
that these conversations are sacred, natural, and most of
all — reciprocal. They hear you. And they want to speak
with you too.

DAY 1

If you could ask your loved one just one question, what would it be?

B egin with curiosity. Questions are invitations. Your inquiry is already being received.

_____

_____

_____

_____

_____

_____

_____

_____

_____

_____

_____

_____

_____

_____

_____

_____

_____

DAY 2

Write a letter to your loved one.
Let it flow without editing.

Your words are a bridge. Trust them. Spirit often answers in the quiet that follows.

_____
_____
_____
_____
_____
_____
_____
_____
_____
_____
_____
_____
_____
_____
_____
_____
_____
_____

DAY 3

Now write a letter from your loved one to you. Don't overthink—just trust what comes.

T heir voice may echo through your own. This is co-creation. Let the pen become a portal.

_____

_____

_____

_____

_____

_____

_____

_____

_____

_____

_____

_____

_____

_____

_____

_____

_____

DAY 4

Sit in stillness for five minutes.
What thoughts or impressions arise?

S tillness makes the subtle more audible. Even quiet moments are filled with presence.

DAY 5

Ask them a question before bed.
Notice your dreams—what themes or
symbols appear?

S pirit often visits through dreams. You may feel it
more than you remember it. Let it come.

_____
_____
_____
_____
_____
_____
_____
_____
_____
_____
_____
_____
_____
_____
_____

DAY 6

What would a "sign" feel like to you today? Invite it without pressurizing it or having to show up a specific way.

L et your heart be the receiver. Signs often speak through feeling, not logic.

_____
_____
_____
_____
_____
_____
_____
_____
_____
_____
_____
_____
_____
_____
_____

DAY 7

Try automatic writing: set a timer for five minutes and let words spill onto the page.

L et go of making sense. Let Spirit move through your hand. There's clarity in the uncensored flow.

_____
_____
_____
_____
_____
_____
_____
_____
_____
_____
_____
_____
_____
_____
_____
_____
_____

DAY 8

If they could reply to your grief, what would they say?

F eel into the wisdom already living in your heart. Their reply may be softer than words.

_____
_____
_____
_____
_____
_____
_____
_____
_____
_____
_____
_____
_____
_____
_____
_____

DAY 9

What's one phrase or quote that always reminds you of them? Write it and sit with it.

F amiliar words carry frequency. Let them open the space between you.

_____
_____
_____
_____
_____
_____
_____
_____
_____
_____
_____
_____
_____
_____
_____
_____
_____

DAY 10

Close your eyes and picture their face.
What do you hear or feel in their presence?

Their image is a doorway. Let it open slowly. Let it fill the space with feeling.

_____

_____

_____

_____

_____

_____

_____

_____

_____

_____

_____

_____

_____

_____

_____

_____

DAY 11

Choose an object that belonged to them or reminds you of them. If you have it in physical form, hold it. If not, picture it. What emotions or messages surface?

✦

Objects can carry energetic residue — sacred echoes. Let sensation speak and trust what comes up.

_____
_____
_____
_____
_____
_____
_____
_____
_____
_____
_____
_____
_____

DAY 12

Speak to them out loud today.
What feels different afterward?

Your voice carries love across realms. Even if it feels one-sided, Spirit always listens.

DAY 13

*If they had a message for you today,
what do you think it would be? Trust your
first thought.*

S pirit speaks in the whispers we almost dismiss. That
subtle thought you keep brushing away? It may be
them.

_____

_____

_____

_____

_____

_____

_____

_____

_____

_____

_____

_____

_____

_____

DAY 14

Have you ever received a message you dismissed? Revisit it now.

G ive yourself permission to believe it mattered. You may hear more this time around.

DAY 15

Ask a yes/no question, then sit quietly.
What answer do you feel in your body?

L et your body become the tuning fork. What feels light, what feels heavy? Spirit often answers through subtle sensation.

_____

_____

_____

_____

_____

_____

_____

_____

_____

_____

_____

_____

_____

_____

_____

DAY 16

Imagine having coffee or tea with them.
What would the conversation be like?

Create a mental space of warmth and presence.
Their energy may arrive in feelings or memory.

_____

_____

_____

_____

_____

_____

_____

_____

_____

_____

_____

_____

_____

_____

_____

_____

_____

_____

DAY 17

If your loved one had a nickname or special phrase for you, write it now. How does it feel to see it again?

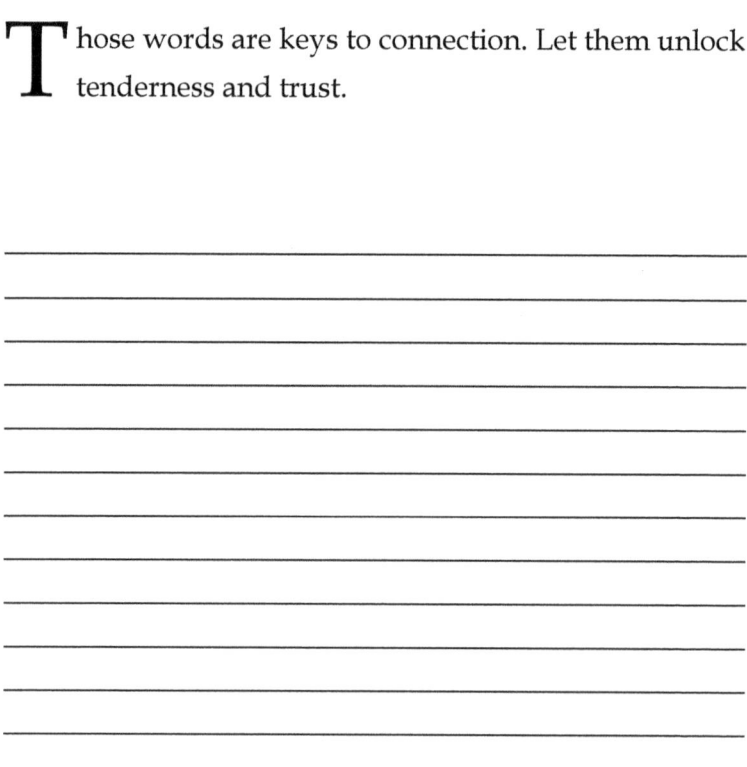

T hose words are keys to connection. Let them unlock tenderness and trust.

DAY 18

Ask your loved one to help you with something specific today.
Watch what unfolds.

L et them into your day-to-day. They often show up in small, meaningful ways.

_____
_____
_____
_____
_____
_____
_____
_____
_____
_____
_____
_____
_____
_____
_____

DAY 19

*What would it look like to let them finish
a sentence you begin? Try this now.*

S tart with "Today I would like…" and listen. Let
their voice meet you in the in-between.

_____

_____

_____

_____

_____

_____

_____

_____

_____

_____

_____

_____

_____

_____

_____

_____

_____

_____

DAY 20

Have you ever had a conversation in your head that felt like it wasn't just you? Describe it.

That voice may not be your imagination—it may be intuition. Spirit speaks within your own inner tone.

_____

_____

_____

_____

_____

_____

_____

_____

_____

_____

_____

_____

_____

_____

_____

_____

DAY 21

Revisit an old voicemail, letter, or memory. What new message do you receive from it now?

M essages can evolve as we do. What was once overlooked may now hold deep meaning.

DAY 22

What does their soul feel like to you now?
What qualities do they carry in Spirit?

F eel beyond memory. Their essence has expanded.
Let their spirit meet you as it is now.

_____
_____
_____
_____
_____
_____
_____
_____
_____
_____
_____
_____
_____
_____
_____
_____

DAY 23

Is there a part of you that doubts their presence? What would it take to begin to trust?

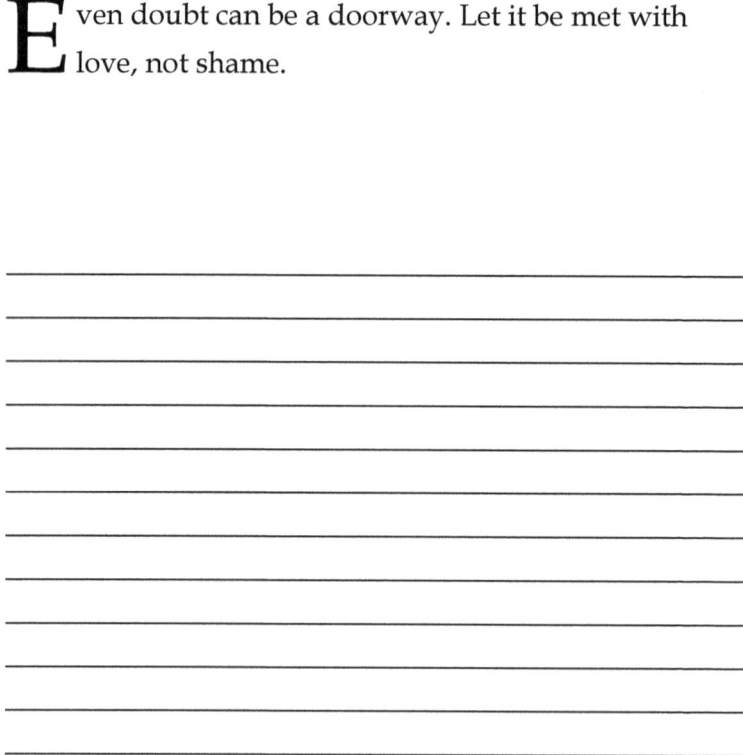

E ven doubt can be a doorway. Let it be met with love, not shame.

_____
_____
_____
_____
_____
_____
_____
_____
_____
_____
_____
_____
_____

DAY 24

Imagine them whispering one sentence of encouragement to you. What is it?

R eceive the sentence without judgment. It might be
exactly what you've needed to hear.

_____

_____

_____

_____

_____

_____

_____

_____

_____

_____

_____

_____

_____

_____

_____

DAY 25

Record a voice note speaking to them.
Listen back later—how does it feel?

Your voice carries a vibration of love. Let it echo
back to your heart.

_____

_____

_____

_____

_____

_____

_____

_____

_____

_____

_____

_____

_____

_____

_____

_____

DAY 26

Ask them to help you with a choice or decision today. What guidance arises?

Their answer may arrive through peace, clarity, or timing. Spirit guides through resonance.

_____

_____

_____

_____

_____

_____

_____

_____

_____

_____

_____

_____

_____

_____

_____

_____

DAY 27

*Do you ever feel a presence behind or
beside you? Explore what that feels like.*

✦

S pirit often stands just to the side — quiet, steady,
near. Let yourself acknowledge it, even if it's subtle.

_____

_____

_____

_____

_____

_____

_____

_____

_____

_____

_____

_____

_____

_____

_____

DAY 28

*What signs or messages have felt too quiet
to trust—but too meaningful to ignore?*

Not every whisper from beyond will come with proof. Let resonance be your recognition.

_____
_____
_____
_____
_____
_____
_____
_____
_____
_____
_____
_____
_____
_____
_____
_____
_____
_____

DAY 29

What emotions arise when you sense their presence near you?

Y ou don't have to question whether it's real. Let
yourself feel it, exactly as it is.

_____
_____
_____
_____
_____
_____
_____
_____
_____
_____
_____
_____
_____
_____
_____
_____

DAY 30

*What has this month shown you about
how Spirit speaks to you?*

T he veil is thinner than it seems. Let this relationship
continue, in the language only you share.

_____
_____
_____
_____
_____
_____
_____
_____
_____
_____
_____
_____
_____
_____
_____
_____
_____

MONTH FIVE

The Body Remembers

G rief doesn't live only in the heart—it lives in the body. It settles in the shoulders, the chest, the stomach. It shows up as fatigue, tension, restlessness, or a sudden wave of emotion.

This month, we turn inward and listen to the physical intelligence of grief. Your body remembers love, loss, presence, and Spirit. It also knows how to release and renew.

I'll be here with you, encouraging you to treat your body with tenderness, to feel instead of force, and to discover that your physical form can also be a sacred bridge to connection.

DAY 1

Where do you feel grief in your body today? Name the place without judgment.

Your body is not betraying you — it's holding the imprint of your love. Let that place be seen, softened, and honored.

DAY 2

When you think of your loved one, where do you feel warmth, light, or peace?

These sensations are often Spirit's quiet ways of staying near. Trust the warmth. It's them.

_____

_____

_____

_____

_____

_____

_____

_____

_____

_____

_____

_____

_____

_____

_____

_____

_____

DAY 3

*Take three deep breaths. What rises
to the surface?*

B reath reveals what's been waiting beneath. Let it
rise without needing to fix it.

_____
_____
_____
_____
_____
_____
_____
_____
_____
_____
_____
_____
_____
_____
_____
_____

DAY 4

Describe your energy levels lately. Are you tired, wired, grounded?

✦

G rief rewrites the rhythms of our body. Let yourself move at the pace your soul requires.

_____

_____

_____

_____

_____

_____

_____

_____

_____

_____

_____

_____

_____

_____

_____

_____

DAY 5

*What physical action helps you release
emotion most easily?*

M ovement and stillness both become medicine
when they're made sacred. Cry, walk, dance, or
be still—Spirit can meet you in all of it.

_____

_____

_____

_____

_____

_____

_____

_____

_____

_____

_____

_____

_____

_____

_____

_____

DAY 6

Place your hand over your heart.
What do you hear or feel?

This small act is a portal. Spirit often sends peace through sensation. Let your own hand become the comfort you seek.

_____
_____
_____
_____
_____
_____
_____
_____
_____
_____
_____
_____
_____
_____
_____
_____
_____

DAY 7

*Have you had any unusual physical
sensations since their passing?
Explore what they might mean.*

Goosebumps, warmth, chills — these can be your
body's acknowledgment of Spirit. Let your body
become your partner.

_____

_____

_____

_____

_____

_____

_____

_____

_____

_____

_____

_____

_____

_____

DAY 8

What part of your body is asking for more care or attention right now?

Bring love to that place. Touch it gently. Breathe with it. This is tending. This is healing.

_____

_____

_____

_____

_____

_____

_____

_____

_____

_____

_____

_____

_____

_____

_____

_____

_____

_____

DAY 9

How has your sleep changed since this transition? What do you notice in the quiet hours?

The night often holds more than rest. Let it become a space for integration.

_____

_____

_____

_____

_____

_____

_____

_____

_____

_____

_____

_____

_____

_____

_____

DAY 10

Describe what it feels like when you sense your loved one is near, if you do. What happens physically?

Y ou may feel a shift, a stillness, a subtle tingle. Let those sensations be real.

_____

_____

_____

_____

_____

_____

_____

_____

_____

_____

_____

_____

_____

_____

_____

DAY 11

Take a slow walk today and notice what your body is telling you.

G rief can settle in our legs, our chest, our breath. Let each step be a release, a reverence.

_____
_____
_____
_____
_____
_____
_____
_____
_____
_____
_____
_____
_____
_____
_____
_____
_____
_____

DAY 12

Create a ritual of touch—massage your hands, hold your heart, place a blanket over your shoulders.

Y our body is worthy of tenderness. These acts of care invite Spirit closer.

_____
_____
_____
_____
_____
_____
_____
_____
_____
_____
_____
_____
_____
_____
_____
_____
_____
_____

DAY 13

What posture do you naturally take when you're grieving? What might that posture be protecting?

C urled shoulders, lowered gaze — your body is protecting your heart. Let that be okay. You are worthy of gentleness.

_____
_____
_____
_____
_____
_____
_____
_____
_____
_____
_____
_____
_____

DAY 14

Stretch gently. Where do you feel resistance? Where do you feel release?

✦

Stretching opens space for what has been held too long. Let the breath follow the release.

DAY 15

Do you carry physical objects that remind you of them? What do you feel when you hold them?

Th ese items carry memory and sometimes presence. Let them be more than things — let them be thresholds.

_____
_____
_____
_____
_____
_____
_____
_____
_____
_____
_____
_____
_____
_____

DAY 16

What foods or smells remind you of them?
How does your body react?

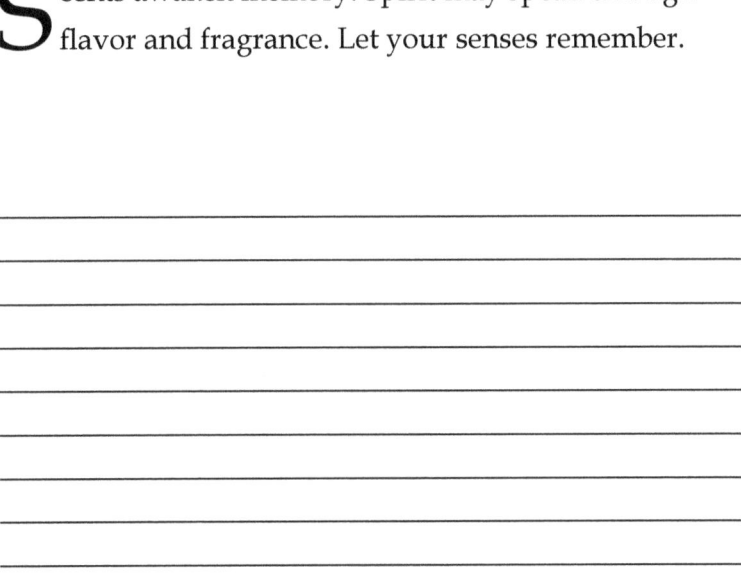

S cents awaken memory. Spirit may speak through
flavor and fragrance. Let your senses remember.

_____

_____

_____

_____

_____

_____

_____

_____

_____

_____

_____

_____

_____

_____

DAY 17

How has your relationship with your body
changed since they passed?

✦

G rief reshapes even our embodiment. Let this be a
season of renewed connection.

_____

_____

_____

_____

_____

_____

_____

_____

_____

_____

_____

_____

_____

_____

_____

_____

_____

DAY 18

Create a body blessing. Speak kindness over each part of you that's held pain.

B less your shoulders, your feet, your belly. Thank them. Your body has done holy work.

_____
_____
_____
_____
_____
_____
_____
_____
_____
_____
_____
_____
_____
_____
_____
_____

DAY 19

Have you felt more intuitive or sensitive
since your loss? How does it feel physically?

S ensitivity is how Spirit touches the world through
you. It will naturally integrate as you allow it.

_____

_____

_____

_____

_____

_____

_____

_____

_____

_____

_____

_____

_____

_____

_____

_____

DAY 20

Do you get "gut feelings" about your loved one's presence? Where do you feel them?

Your intuition lives in your tissues. The gut, the chest, the skin — they're all listening.

_____
_____
_____
_____
_____
_____
_____
_____
_____
_____
_____
_____
_____
_____
_____
_____
_____
_____

DAY 21

Do you move through your grief or does it sit still inside of you? What does it want?

B oth are valid. Motion and stillness can both be sacred. Ask what your grief needs today.

_____
_____
_____
_____
_____
_____
_____
_____
_____
_____
_____
_____
_____
_____
_____
_____
_____
_____

DAY 22

*Try humming or chanting softly.
What vibrations do you feel?*

Your voice is a tuning fork. Let it shift your
frequency. This is sound as soul medicine.

DAY 23

*Have you experienced a physical release
after a cry or spiritual moment?
What did it feel like?*

L et the tears be teachers. Often what follows is
lightness, warmth, clarity, rest.

_____

_____

_____

_____

_____

_____

_____

_____

_____

_____

_____

_____

_____

_____

DAY 24

*What small movement could you make
today as a gesture of healing?*

A breath. A bow. A stretch. A step outside. Even a
tiny shift opens the field.

_____

_____

_____

_____

_____

_____

_____

_____

_____

_____

_____

_____

_____

_____

_____

_____

DAY 25

Does your grief feel heavy or light today?
Where do you feel that weight?

Bring your attention there with love. You don't need to carry it alone.

_____
_____
_____
_____
_____
_____
_____
_____
_____
_____
_____
_____
_____
_____
_____
_____

DAY 26

Use your voice—speak their name aloud.
How does your body respond?

Their name is a key. Say it like a prayer and notice
what stirs.

_____

_____

_____

_____

_____

_____

_____

_____

_____

_____

_____

_____

_____

_____

_____

_____

_____

_____

DAY 27

Have you felt physical shifts during
prayer, meditation, or spiritual moments?

✦

A wave of energy, a deep exhale, a stillness — that's
Spirit. Your body is part of the conversation.

_____
_____
_____
_____
_____
_____
_____
_____
_____
_____
_____
_____
_____
_____
_____
_____

DAY 28

Place your feet on the ground and imagine energy moving through you. What do you notice?

Feel your body in communion with the Earth. Let her hold you. Grief, too, is a current of connection.

_____

_____

_____

_____

_____

_____

_____

_____

_____

_____

_____

_____

_____

_____

_____

DAY 29

What does your body want to feel more of—touch, warmth, rest, movement? Listen and respond.

Your body is not separate from your soul—it's a sacred vessel. Give it what it's quietly asking for.

_____

_____

_____

_____

_____

_____

_____

_____

_____

_____

_____

_____

_____

_____

_____

_____

_____

DAY 30

What does your body know now that it didn't before your loss?

G rief reshapes the body as much as the heart. Let your healing be embodied, not just understood.

_____

_____

_____

_____

_____

_____

_____

_____

_____

_____

_____

_____

_____

_____

_____

MONTH SIX

Signs, Symbols, and Sacred Visits

S pirit is always communicating—but not always in words. Our loved ones often speak to us through subtle signs, animals, flickering lights, familiar scents, dreams, and unexpected synchronicities. These moments aren't coincidences—they are love letters from the other side.

This month, we'll deepen your awareness of the signs that are already around you. I'll help you recognize, trust, and receive these messages as real and sacred. You're not imagining it—Spirit is reaching out. And you're learning how to listen.

DAY 1

*What's one sign you've received that felt
too meaningful to ignore?
Describe it in detail.*

T hat wasn't random. Spirit speaks through
resonance. Let that moment come alive again in
your heart—it may still be whispering to you.

_____

_____

_____

_____

_____

_____

_____

_____

_____

_____

_____

_____

_____

_____

_____

_____

DAY 2

Have you ever seen repeating numbers (like 1111 or 444)? What were you thinking about at the time?

Numbers are cosmic nudges—Spirit's shorthand for expansion and alignment beyond outgrown frameworks. Notice what surrounds the number. It's part of the message.

_____

_____

_____

_____

_____

_____

_____

_____

_____

_____

_____

_____

_____

_____

_____

DAY 3

If your loved one could choose a symbol,
an animal, a song to represent themselves,
what would it be?

Y ou may already know this symbol deep down.
Naming it opens a channel. Notice as it shows up
in your life.

_____

_____

_____

_____

_____

_____

_____

_____

_____

_____

_____

_____

_____

_____

_____

DAY 4

What song seems to follow you lately, and what might it be saying?

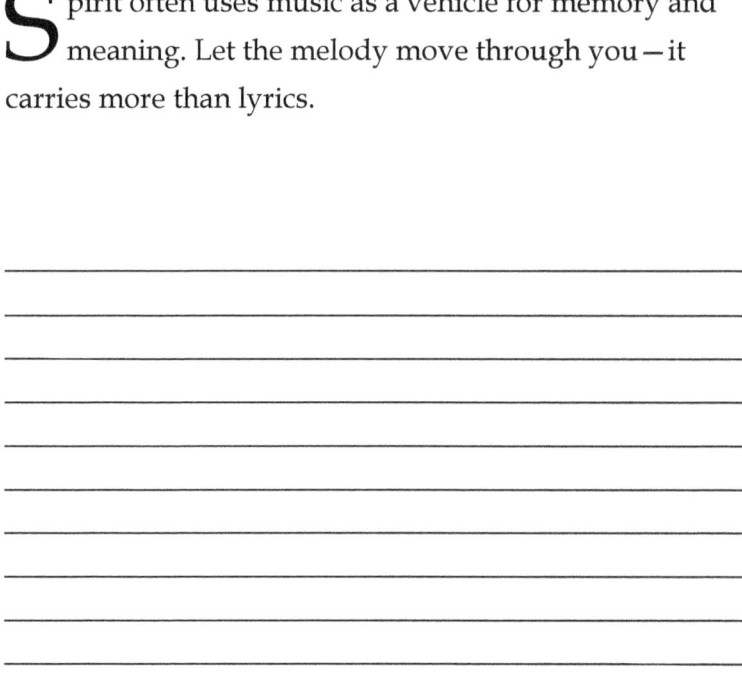

S pirit often uses music as a vehicle for memory and meaning. Let the melody move through you — it carries more than lyrics.

_____

_____

_____

_____

_____

_____

_____

_____

_____

_____

_____

_____

_____

_____

_____

DAY 5

Has an animal ever appeared at an interesting time? What did you feel in that moment?

S pirit loves to collaborate with nature. Birds, butterflies, dragonflies — they all carry messages. Let your heart feel what words can't explain.

_____

_____

_____

_____

_____

_____

_____

_____

_____

_____

_____

_____

_____

DAY 6

Describe a dream that felt like more than just a dream. What stood out, what do you sense?

Visitation dreams bring peace, clarity, and presence. Let your dream memory become a portal, not a question.

_____
_____
_____
_____
_____
_____
_____
_____
_____
_____
_____
_____
_____
_____
_____
_____

DAY 7

Have you ever noticed a sudden breeze or a gentle shift in the air while thinking of them?

✦

S pirit sometimes speaks through sensation. The air itself can become a messenger. Sense into what moved in that moment—and what moved in you.

DAY 8

What object or keepsake carries their energy? Hold it—what do you sense?

O bjects hold vibration. They can hum with presence. Let this object become a reminder of love.

_____
_____
_____
_____
_____
_____
_____
_____
_____
_____
_____
_____
_____
_____

DAY 9

*If you asked for a sign today, what would
you want it to be? Ask—and stay open.*

Your request is a door opening. Spirit responds
in both subtle and dramatic ways. Release the
pressure for performance and allow.

DAY 10

Have you experienced technology acting oddly around you—phones, lights, radios?

E lectronics are easy tools to reach you. Those flickers may be winks through the veil.

_____
_____
_____
_____
_____
_____
_____
_____
_____
_____
_____
_____
_____
_____
_____
_____
_____
_____

DAY 11

What natural elements remind you of them—water, wind, trees, stars? What might they be saying through these?

N ature is Spirit's poetry. Let the elements carry their voice in ways your soul understands.

_____
_____
_____
_____
_____
_____
_____
_____
_____
_____
_____
_____
_____
_____
_____
_____
_____

DAY 12

Have you ever felt someone touching your
hair, shoulder, or hand when
no one was there?

T hat's not your imagination — it's presence in its
gentlest form. Spirit often speaks in sensation.

_____
_____
_____
_____
_____
_____
_____
_____
_____
_____
_____
_____
_____
_____
_____
_____

DAY 13

*What does "feeling their presence" mean
to you? When has it happened?*

Presence is a felt frequency — peace, emotion,
warmth. Let your definition be enough.

_____

_____

_____

_____

_____

_____

_____

_____

_____

_____

_____

_____

_____

_____

_____

DAY 14

If they could leave you a sign in the sky,
what would it look like? Watch today.
You may be surprised.

✦

Clouds, light patterns, rainbows — Spirit loves wonder. Look up with intention and softness.

_____
_____
_____
_____
_____
_____
_____
_____
_____
_____
_____
_____
_____
_____
_____
_____
_____

DAY 15

Have you ever had a sudden burst of emotion with no explanation? What might have triggered it?

T hat wave may have been Spirit coming close. Emotion is often the soul recognizing presence.

_____

_____

_____

_____

_____

_____

_____

_____

_____

_____

_____

_____

_____

_____

_____

DAY 16

What number, color, or phrase reminds you of them? Keep a "sign journal" this week.

Honoring signs builds trust. Patterns may begin to emerge. Let your journal become a map of connection.

_____
_____
_____
_____
_____
_____
_____
_____
_____
_____
_____
_____
_____
_____
_____
_____
_____
_____

DAY 17

Have you ever been "guided" to something unexpectedly—a book, a message, a place? What happened?

S ynchronicity is Spirit's choreography. Follow the thread. It's leading somewhere meaningful.

_____
_____
_____
_____
_____
_____
_____
_____
_____
_____
_____
_____
_____
_____
_____
_____

DAY 18

Ask your loved one for a dream visit.
What message would you like to receive?

S peak it aloud. Set the invitation with intension and clarity. Then rest and receive.

_____

_____

_____

_____

_____

_____

_____

_____

_____

_____

_____

_____

_____

_____

_____

DAY 19

Write about a time you knew they were near, even if others didn't understand.

Y ou don't need anyone else to validate what you felt. Your knowing is sacred.

_____
_____
_____
_____
_____
_____
_____
_____
_____
_____
_____
_____
_____
_____
_____
_____

DAY 20

Have you ever seen something in nature that looked like a symbol or message? Describe it.

Nature becomes a mirror when Spirit is speaking. Describe the sign as if it were written just for you—it was.

_____
_____
_____
_____
_____
_____
_____
_____
_____
_____
_____
_____
_____
_____
_____
_____

DAY 21

Create a sign together. Say, "When I see [___], I'll know you're near." Then wait.

✦

This is co-creation. Spirit loves agreement and intention. Your sign will come when your heart is open.

_____
_____
_____
_____
_____
_____
_____
_____
_____
_____
_____
_____
_____
_____
_____
_____
_____
_____

DAY 22

What is your favorite sign you've received so far? How did it make you feel?

Revisit that moment. It's a touchstone now. Let it comfort you again.

_____

_____

_____

_____

_____

_____

_____

_____

_____

_____

_____

_____

_____

_____

_____

DAY 23

*Have you ever been thinking about them
and suddenly felt them with you?
What were you doing?*

✦

L ove is the magnet. Your remembering draws them
near. Let that moment anchor your trust.

_____

_____

_____

_____

_____

_____

_____

_____

_____

_____

_____

_____

_____

_____

_____

_____

DAY 24

What would you say to them if they sent you a sign right now? Say it out loud.

S peaking opens the channel even wider. Let the words fly like prayer.

_____

_____

_____

_____

_____

_____

_____

_____

_____

_____

_____

_____

_____

_____

_____

_____

DAY 25

Do lights flicker or turn off/on near you?
What might your loved one be saying in
that moment?

Sometimes Spirit is simply saying, "Hi, I'm here." Talk back. They're listening.

_____

_____

_____

_____

_____

_____

_____

_____

_____

_____

_____

_____

_____

_____

DAY 26

Imagine they're placing a hand on your back or shoulder. What does your body feel?

C lose your eyes. Receive it. That sensation may be their way of staying close.

_____
_____
_____
_____
_____
_____
_____
_____
_____
_____
_____
_____
_____
_____
_____
_____

DAY 27

Have you ever felt time slow down or
speed up during a spiritual moment?

S pirit operates outside of linear time. When you feel
the shift, let it hold you. You've stepped into sacred
space.

_____

_____

_____

_____

_____

_____

_____

_____

_____

_____

_____

_____

_____

_____

_____

_____

_____

DAY 28

Think of a holiday or anniversary when a sign showed up. What do you believe it meant?

T hey remember your shared sacred days. Let their love mark the calendar with presence.

DAY 29

Are you worried that you aren't getting signs, or might be missing them? Sometimes our grief doesn't leave space for noticing.

✦

Stay open. Don't rush. Spirit honors the invitation. Give yourself more grace.

_____

_____

_____

_____

_____

_____

_____

_____

_____

_____

_____

_____

_____

_____

_____

DAY 30

The more you depressurize yourself and open to deep rest, the more you receive. What are you open to seeing today?

L et your rest be the bridge. The smallest sign becomes sacred when your heart says yes.

_____
_____
_____
_____
_____
_____
_____
_____
_____
_____
_____
_____
_____
_____

MONTH SEVEN

Love is the Bridge

G rief and love are two sides of the same coin. You grieve deeply because you loved deeply — and that love doesn't end just because your loved one is no longer in physical form. In fact, love is the very bridge that keeps you connected across the veil.

In this chapter, we'll open from pain into presence, focusing on the bond that continues, the connection that endures, and the love that remains. I'll walk with you through these reflections, gently helping you trust that what you feel is real — and that love, not loss, is the final word.

DAY 1

Recall a moment when you felt loved by them. What do you remember most?

T hat feeling is timeless. Let it rise again in your heart, just as alive now as it was then. Love never leaves — it becomes your inner compass.

DAY 2

If love could speak through your heart today, what would it say?

L et love borrow your voice. These may be their words, rising through you. Love speaks in the language of soul.

_____
_____
_____
_____
_____
_____
_____
_____
_____
_____
_____
_____
_____
_____
_____
_____
_____
_____

DAY 3

Write about how your love for them has evolved since their passing.

✦

L ove does not disappear — it expands. Let your words reveal the way love continues to grow.

_____

_____

_____

_____

_____

_____

_____

_____

_____

_____

_____

_____

_____

_____

_____

_____

_____

_____

DAY 4

*What is one way you still show them
love today?*

L ight a candle, speak their name, carry them in
your choices. Love offered now is just as real—
and always received.

_____
_____
_____
_____
_____
_____
_____
_____
_____
_____
_____
_____
_____
_____
_____

DAY 5

Imagine holding their hand. What does it feel like? What emotion comes through?

L et memory become a bridge to presence. Their touch may rise in sensation, warmth, or tears.

_____
_____
_____
_____
_____
_____
_____
_____
_____
_____
_____
_____
_____
_____
_____
_____
_____

DAY 6

Write a letter beginning with:
"My love for you..."

L et the pen carry your heart. These words stretch across time and space.

_____

_____

_____

_____

_____

_____

_____

_____

_____

_____

_____

_____

_____

_____

_____

_____

DAY 7

When was the last time you smiled or laughed because of a memory of them?

J oy is a return to connection. Let it come without guilt—this is love shining through.

_____
_____
_____
_____
_____
_____
_____
_____
_____
_____
_____
_____
_____
_____
_____
_____

DAY 8

Describe your relationship in one word.
Then write about what that word
means now.

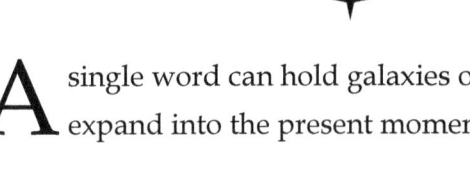

A single word can hold galaxies of memory. Let it expand into the present moment.

_____
_____
_____
_____
_____
_____
_____
_____
_____
_____
_____
_____
_____
_____
_____

DAY 9

*What would they want you to know
about how they feel now?*

Spirit speaks clearly: "I'm okay. I'm free. I'm still
with you." Let these words settle gently in your
chest.

_____

_____

_____

_____

_____

_____

_____

_____

_____

_____

_____

_____

_____

_____

_____

DAY 10

*If you could send them love across the veil,
how would you do it? A prayer, song, ritual?*

S end it in any form that feels sacred. They will feel it,
every time.

_____

_____

_____

_____

_____

_____

_____

_____

_____

_____

_____

_____

_____

_____

_____

_____

_____

DAY 11

When do you feel the most connected to
them? What are you doing?
Are you with others?

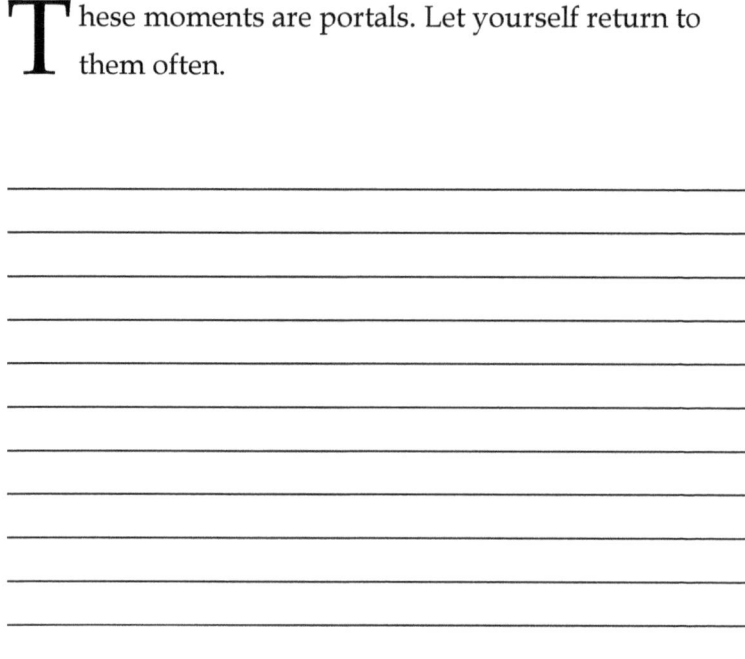

T hese moments are portals. Let yourself return to
them often.

_____

_____

_____

_____

_____

_____

_____

_____

_____

_____

_____

_____

_____

_____

_____

DAY 12

Finish the sentence: "I carry you with me when I..."

T his is how love walks with you — in your living, in your becoming. Let the sentence guide your next steps.

_____

_____

_____

_____

_____

_____

_____

_____

_____

_____

_____

_____

_____

_____

_____

_____

_____

DAY 13

What is something you learned about love because of them?

G rief births wisdom, and love becomes the teacher. Let this lesson root into your soul.

_____
_____
_____
_____
_____
_____
_____
_____
_____
_____
_____
_____
_____
_____
_____
_____
_____

DAY 14

Write about a place that holds love-filled memories of them. What does your heart feel there?

The land remembers. Let that place hold you in return. Love lingers in places where it was once poured freely.

_____

_____

_____

_____

_____

_____

_____

_____

_____

_____

_____

_____

_____

_____

DAY 15

*If you could create a "Love List" of
everything they gave you emotionally,
what would it include?*

L et gratitude lead. Every item on your list is an
energy thread that still connects you. This becomes
a love letter in reverse.

_____

_____

_____

_____

_____

_____

_____

_____

_____

_____

_____

_____

_____

_____

_____

_____

DAY 16

What does unconditional love mean to you now? How has it changed through grief?

L oss tests and expands our capacity to love without condition. Let this love become a steady light.

_____

_____

_____

_____

_____

_____

_____

_____

_____

_____

_____

_____

_____

_____

_____

_____

_____

_____

DAY 17

How did they love you differently than anyone else has?

Their unique love carved a space inside you. It still lives there.

_____

_____

_____

_____

_____

_____

_____

_____

_____

_____

_____

_____

_____

_____

_____

_____

DAY 18

Describe a moment you felt their love
after their passing. What was happening?

Y ou were not imagining it. Let the memory
become a message. That was presence — not just
remembrance.

_____
_____
_____
_____
_____
_____
_____
_____
_____
_____
_____
_____
_____
_____
_____
_____
_____

DAY 19

Write about something you continue to do today that they would be proud of.

Their joy travels with you. You are living a continuation of the love you shared.

_____
_____
_____
_____
_____
_____
_____
_____
_____
_____
_____
_____
_____
_____
_____
_____

DAY 20

What would love do today if it were
guiding your choices?

L et love lead the way — it knows how to find them.
Every loving choice strengthens your connection.

_____

_____
_____
_____
_____
_____
_____
_____
_____
_____
_____
_____
_____
_____
_____
_____
_____

DAY 21

Create a small ritual to send them love.
What does it look like?

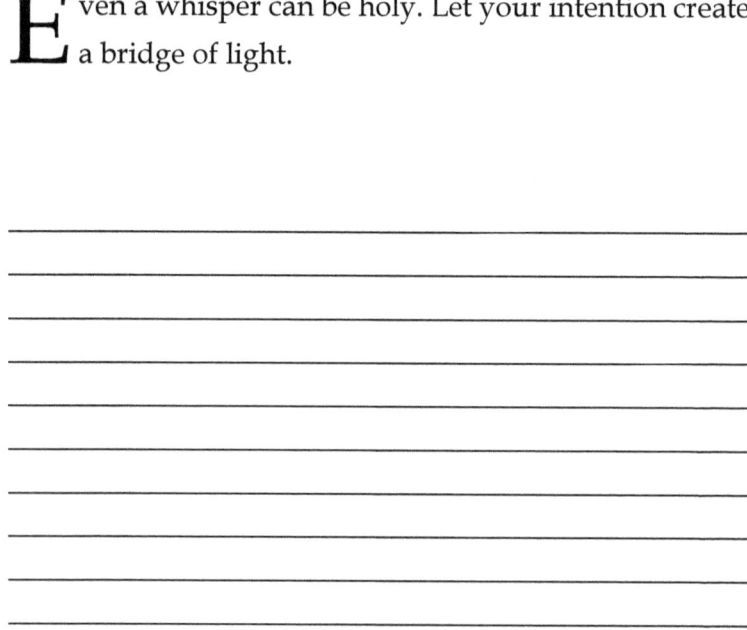

E ven a whisper can be holy. Let your intention create
a bridge of light.

_____

_____

_____

_____

_____

_____

_____

_____

_____

_____

_____

_____

_____

_____

_____

_____

DAY 22

Have you ever felt them when you needed love most? Describe that moment.

Their energy often rises when your heart breaks open. They show up in the quiet, when you're most receptive.

_____

_____

_____

_____

_____

_____

_____

_____

_____

_____

_____

_____

_____

_____

_____

_____

_____

DAY 23

Imagine them in the room with you. What do you notice?

L et your body answer before your mind does. This energy is love remembering you.

_____

_____

_____

_____

_____

_____

_____

_____

_____

_____

_____

_____

_____

_____

_____

_____

_____

DAY 24

*How does grief shift when you focus on
the love that still exists?*

G rief softens when cradled by love. This is not
bypass—it is expansion.

_____

_____

_____

_____

_____

_____

_____

_____

_____

_____

_____

_____

_____

_____

_____

_____

DAY 25

What song, movie, or quote reminds you of the love you shared?

L et it play again. Let the words or notes wrap you in remembrance. Spirit uses these as instruments of connection.

_____

_____

_____

_____

_____

_____

_____

_____

_____

_____

_____

_____

_____

_____

_____

DAY 26

Finish the sentence: "I will always love you through..."

L et the sentence become your vow, your practice, your breath. Love becomes the path you walk.

_____

_____

_____

_____

_____

_____

_____

_____

_____

_____

_____

_____

_____

_____

_____

_____

_____

DAY 27

How do you think they send you love now?
Through what means or messengers?

Signs, dreams, sensations—love finds its way. Let your inner knowing guide you.

_____

_____

_____

_____

_____

_____

_____

_____

_____

_____

_____

_____

_____

_____

_____

_____

DAY 28

Write a vow to continue loving them in ways that bring healing to both of you.

L ove that heals is a two-way current. Let your vow become a daily rhythm.

_____

_____

_____

_____

_____

_____

_____

_____

_____

_____

_____

_____

_____

_____

_____

_____

_____

_____

DAY 29

Imagine them saying: "I love you." How
do you receive it today?

F eel it land in your heart, warm and clear. Let it
become the truth you walk with.

DAY 30

You are not alone. This love, this bond, this presence—you carry it within you. What does that truth mean today?

L et this knowing hold you. You are the embodiment of love continuing. And I am here with you—every step, every remembering.

_____
_____
_____
_____
_____
_____
_____
_____
_____
_____
_____
_____
_____
_____
_____

MONTH EIGHT

You Are Not Alone

G rief can feel isolating — like you're moving through a world that has kept turning while yours has paused. But I want to remind you: you are not alone. Not in your emotions. Not in your memories. And certainly not in Spirit.

This month is an invitation to reconnect — with yourself, with others who understand, and with your loved one who is still with you, just in a new form. As a psychic medium, I can tell you with certainty — your beloved is close, and you are surrounded by more love and support than you may realize. Let this chapter be your soft place to land.

DAY 1

When have you felt most alone in your grief? Did anything help, even a little?

B ringing light to isolation softens its grip. Even in your solitude, Spirit was beside you, listening.

_____

_____

_____

_____

_____

_____

_____

_____

_____

_____

_____

_____

_____

_____

_____

_____

DAY 2

Is there someone in your life who truly gets your grief, even if they've never been through it? Write about them.

S ometimes the soul just knows how to witness another. Their presence may be part of your sacred support team.

_____

_____

_____

_____

_____

_____

_____

_____

_____

_____

_____

_____

_____

_____

_____

DAY 3

Have you ever called out to your loved one in a hard moment? What happened?

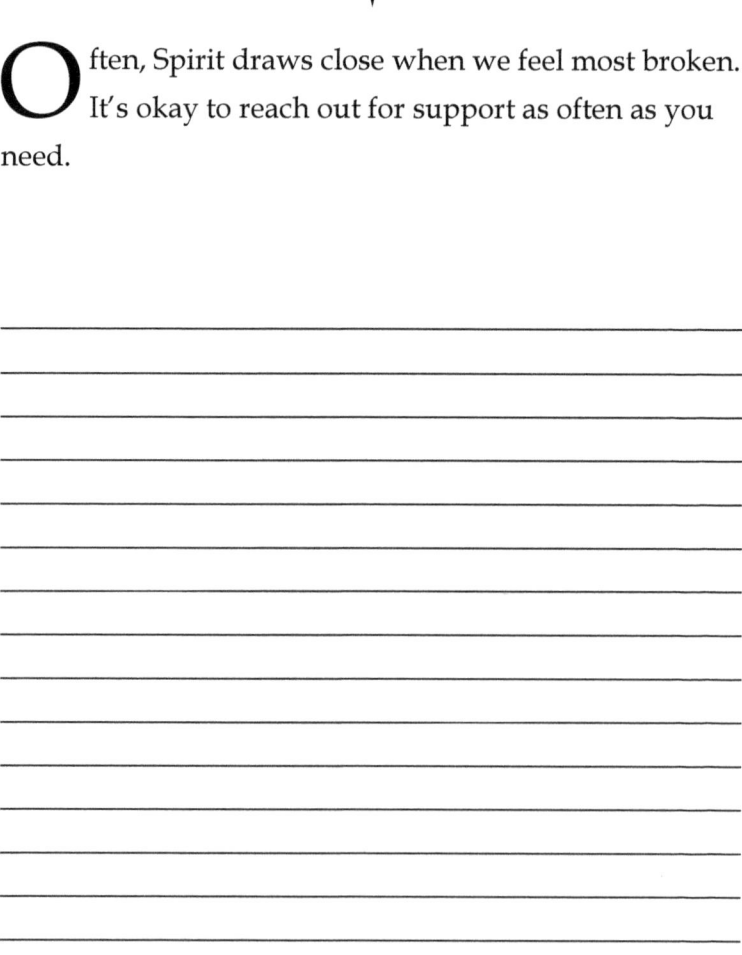

Often, Spirit draws close when we feel most broken. It's okay to reach out for support as often as you need.

_____

_____

_____

_____

_____

_____

_____

_____

_____

_____

_____

_____

_____

_____

_____

DAY 4

*What would it feel like to believe—fully—
that you're being held right now?*

L et that belief become a cloak. This moment can be
your soft place to land.

_____
_____
_____
_____
_____
_____
_____
_____
_____
_____
_____
_____
_____
_____
_____

DAY 5

Write a letter to someone you wish would support you better. Let your truth out.

T hese words aren't for blame — they're for release.
Your grief deserves to be acknowledged.

_____

_____

_____

_____

_____

_____

_____

_____

_____

_____

_____

_____

_____

_____

_____

_____

_____

_____

DAY 6

What would your loved one want you to know about being alone?

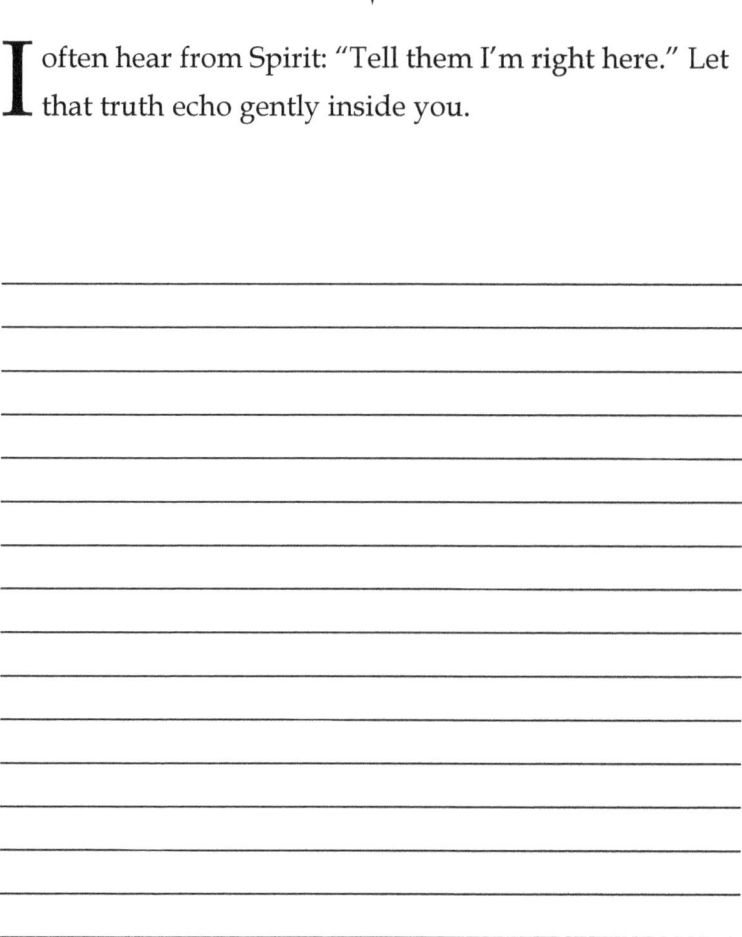

I often hear from Spirit: "Tell them I'm right here." Let that truth echo gently inside you.

_____

_____

_____

_____

_____

_____

_____

_____

_____

_____

_____

_____

_____

_____

_____

DAY 7

What support have you been afraid to ask for? What's holding you back?

Y ou don't need to do this alone. Let receiving be an act of self-honoring.

_____

_____

_____

_____

_____

_____

_____

_____

_____

_____

_____

_____

_____

_____

_____

_____

_____

DAY 8

Who has shown you unexpected kindness since your loss? Write about that moment.

✦

S pirit often uses people as vessels of comfort. Let that kindness live again through your remembering.

DAY 9

*What is one thing you wish people would
say to you in your grief?*

S peak it now. You deserve those words. Let them
become your new inner dialogue.

_____
_____
_____
_____
_____
_____
_____
_____
_____
_____
_____
_____
_____
_____
_____
_____
_____

DAY 10

What do you believe your loved one is doing in Spirit right now?

They are learning, loving, watching over you. Your bond continues in ways both seen and unseen.

_____
_____
_____
_____
_____
_____
_____
_____
_____
_____
_____
_____
_____
_____
_____
_____
_____
_____

DAY 11

Has your grief deepened your empathy for others? How have you changed?

Y our heart has grown through the pain. Let that softness be your strength.

_____

_____

_____

_____

_____

_____

_____

_____

_____

_____

_____

_____

_____

_____

_____

_____

DAY 12

Do you sense any new spiritual support,
spiritual collaborators or synchronicities?
Describe them.

G rief often opens the door to Spirit. Let your
awareness expand without needing proof.

DAY 13

What would it feel like to be truly comforted, even if nothing could be "fixed"?

C omfort is enough. Allow yourself permission to simply be. You don't have to reach for answers — just let your breath meet the moment.

_____
_____
_____
_____
_____
_____
_____
_____
_____
_____
_____
_____
_____
_____
_____
_____

DAY 14

Who else in your life has experienced deep loss? Is there a connection waiting to be made?

Y ou are not the only one walking this path.
Together, healing can potentially deepen.

_____
_____
_____
_____
_____
_____
_____
_____
_____
_____
_____
_____
_____
_____
_____
_____

DAY 15

What group, book, ritual, animal, place in nature, or spiritual tool has helped you feel less alone?

These are your anchors. Return to what steadies you. Trust that what comforted you once may comfort you again.

_____
_____
_____
_____
_____
_____
_____
_____
_____
_____
_____
_____
_____
_____

DAY 16

Imagine your loved one sitting with you on a bench. What do they say to remind you you're not alone?

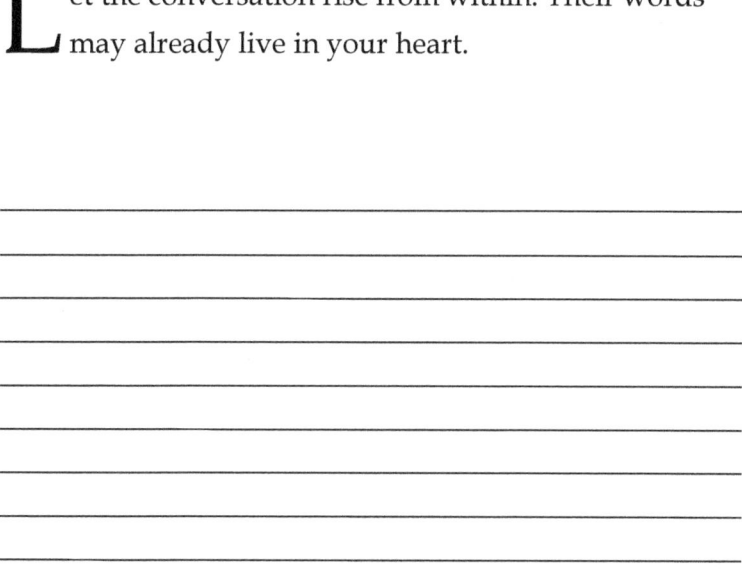

L et the conversation rise from within. Their words may already live in your heart.

_____

_____

_____

_____

_____

_____

_____

_____

_____

_____

_____

_____

_____

_____

_____

_____

DAY 17

What would it mean to believe your grief is witnessed—by Spirit, by the universe, by me?

I t means you are seen, even in silence. Let that knowing hold you.

_____

_____

_____

_____

_____

_____

_____

_____

_____

_____

_____

_____

_____

_____

_____

_____

DAY 18

Have you ever cried in a place where no one saw you? What did you need in that moment?

That cry was sacred. Spirit held you in the hidden space. You were not alone, even if no one else knew.

_____
_____
_____
_____
_____
_____
_____
_____
_____
_____
_____
_____
_____
_____
_____
_____

DAY 19

*What words have stayed with you from
someone who tried to help,
even if imperfectly?*

L et the intention matter more than the phrasing.
Even clumsy love is love.

_____

_____

_____

_____

_____

_____

_____

_____

_____

_____

_____

_____

_____

_____

_____

_____

DAY 20

Write a mantra that reminds you you're connected, even in isolation.

✦

Speak it slowly. Let it enter your cells. You are not alone. You are not alone. You are not alone.

_____

_____

_____

_____

_____

_____

_____

_____

_____

_____

_____

_____

_____

_____

_____

_____

DAY 21

Think of someone in your life who needs support too. What could you offer from your well of empathy?

Y ou don't have to give from depletion. Even one gesture can ripple outward.

_____
_____
_____
_____
_____
_____
_____
_____
_____
_____
_____
_____
_____
_____
_____

DAY 22

Have you had a "coincidence" that felt like divine timing? What do you believe it meant?

These alignments are Spirit's choreography. Trust the mystery that leads you.

_____

_____

_____

_____

_____

_____

_____

_____

_____

_____

_____

_____

_____

_____

_____

_____

DAY 23

What does community mean to you now,
after loss? Has your idea of it shifted?

✦

G rief reshapes belonging. Let it lead you to deeper,
truer circles.

_____
_____
_____
_____
_____
_____
_____
_____
_____
_____
_____
_____
_____
_____
_____
_____

DAY 24

*Light a candle for your loved one and say
aloud: "I know you're with me."
What does your body feel?*

T he body often feels what the mind can't name. Let
the flame be a messenger.

_____

_____

_____

_____

_____

_____

_____

_____

_____

_____

_____

_____

_____

_____

DAY 25

*If you could feel held today—by your loved
one, by Spirit, by the universe—what would
you do differently?*

T ry doing one of those things now. Let love support
your next small step.

_____

_____

_____

_____

_____

_____

_____

_____

_____

_____

_____

_____

_____

_____

_____

DAY 26

Who do you need to forgive to feel more free in your relationships? Yourself? Someone else?

✦

F orgiveness clears the debris between you and connection. Let it be a soft letting go.

DAY 27

Imagine a room where all the people who love you—physical and Spirit—are gathered. Who is there?

Y ou may not even have met some of them in this
lifetime. But this room exists. Let yourself return to
it often.

_____
_____
_____
_____
_____
_____
_____
_____
_____
_____
_____
_____
_____
_____

DAY 28

*Create a list called "I Am Supported By…"
and name as many people, energies, and
memories as you can.*

T his list is your invisible web. Read it aloud and let it
remind you: you are held.

_____
_____
_____
_____
_____
_____
_____
_____
_____
_____
_____
_____
_____
_____
_____
_____
_____
_____

DAY 29

If someone reading this book felt just as alone as you have, what would you say to them? Write it.

✦

Y ou may be giving voice to your own healing. Let the words be a healing balm—for both of you.

DAY 30

You are not alone. I'm here with you. Your loved one is with you. And you are being held—right now. What would it feel like to truly receive that?

B reathe into it. Let this moment hold you. This is your turning point. Let it carry you forward.

_____
_____
_____
_____
_____
_____
_____
_____
_____
_____
_____
_____
_____
_____

MONTH NINE

Spirit as a Daily Companion

Your loved one's presence isn't limited to dreams, signs, or ceremonies — it can live inside the everyday. Spirit wants to be part of your life, not just your grief. Whether you're making coffee, walking the dog, journaling, or washing dishes, they can walk beside you in quiet, beautiful ways.

This month is about deepening that everyday relationship. As a medium, I've witnessed how Spirit longs to stay connected, to walk with us, guide us, laugh with us, and remind us: the relationship is not over — it's just transformed. Let's invite them in, together.

DAY 1

What's one ordinary moment where you felt their presence?

Spirit loves the mundane — where your heart is soft and your guard is down. The ordinary is often where their soul slips through.

_____

_____

_____

_____

_____

_____

_____

_____

_____

_____

_____

_____

_____

_____

_____

_____

DAY 2

If you spoke to them out loud today, what would you say? Go ahead—try it now.

Your voice is a bridge. Even your casual words are received with love.

DAY 3

*What is one daily ritual that could
become a space for Spirit—lighting a
candle, making tea, walking?*

L et simplicity be sacred. Even quiet repetition
becomes an altar of connection.

DAY 4

Have you ever caught yourself smiling or laughing because of them? Write about that moment.

T hat joy was shared. It may have been their hello in disguise.

_____

_____

_____

_____

_____

_____

_____

_____

_____

_____

_____

_____

_____

_____

_____

_____

DAY 5

What would it look like to start your day with their love in mind? Try it tomorrow.

B egin with presence. A simple "Good morning" opens the channel.

_____

_____

_____

_____

_____

_____

_____

_____

_____

_____

_____

_____

_____

_____

_____

DAY 6

Write a message to them that you could read aloud each day.

Thishis becomes a daily tether across dimensions. Let your words become a rhythm of remembrance.

_____
_____
_____
_____
_____
_____
_____
_____
_____
_____
_____
_____
_____
_____
_____
_____
_____
_____

DAY 7

*Do you ever feel pulled to share your story
or their memory with someone else?
What happened?*

S ometimes, Spirit nudges us to speak their name
aloud. Telling their story can support you, when it
feels aligned.

_____

_____

_____

_____

_____

_____

_____

_____

_____

_____

_____

_____

_____

_____

_____

_____

DAY 8

What if you asked their advice on something small today? What do you imagine they'd say?

T heir voice may echo through your intuition. Let the conversation unfold in your heart.

_____
_____
_____
_____
_____
_____
_____
_____
_____
_____
_____
_____
_____

DAY 9

Write a short blessing for your morning or evening that includes them.

This blessing can be your invitation, your remembering, your bridge. Let it become a soft spiritual ritual.

_____

_____

_____

_____

_____

_____

_____

_____

_____

_____

_____

_____

_____

_____

_____

DAY 10

When do you feel most "yourself"?

Your authentic self is often where Spirit meets you.
Trust that their love flows through your presence.

_____
_____
_____
_____
_____
_____
_____
_____
_____
_____
_____
_____
_____
_____
_____
_____
_____
_____
_____

DAY 11

What music brings them close to you?
Play it or sing it today.

S ongs are soul threads. Let the sound carry your love
back and forth.

_____

_____
_____
_____
_____
_____
_____
_____
_____
_____
_____
_____
_____
_____
_____
_____

DAY 12

Describe your daily life now. Where might Spirit already be woven in?

Y ou may be walking with them more than you realize. Look again—they may be in the rhythm of your days.

DAY 13

Have you ever been "guided" to say or do something unexpectedly? What happened?

T hat nudge may be their quiet voice. Spirit often moves through your expression.

_____
_____
_____
_____
_____
_____
_____
_____
_____
_____
_____
_____
_____
_____

DAY 14

What would it be like to create a recurring "Spirit check-in" moment each day. What would that look like?

✦

One breath. One pause. One hello. This may support you in balancing your new life.

_____
_____
_____
_____
_____
_____
_____
_____
_____
_____
_____
_____
_____
_____
_____
_____

DAY 15

Write about how you could carry them with you into something new—work, art, relationships.

They are open to be part of your becoming, to the degree that feels supportive to you. They're available to move forward with you.

_____

_____

_____

_____

_____

_____

_____

_____

_____

_____

_____

_____

_____

_____

DAY 16

What would it mean to see your life as shared with them? Not just after death, but now.

T his is the deeper truth. Your relationship is alive in the present tense.

_____
_____
_____
_____
_____
_____
_____
_____
_____
_____
_____
_____
_____
_____
_____
_____

DAY 17

Do you ever speak to them in your mind during the day? What do you say?

That inner voice may be part of the soul-to-soul channel. Let the dialogue keep flowing, as long as it feels supportive for you.

_____
_____
_____
_____
_____
_____
_____
_____
_____
_____
_____
_____
_____
_____
_____
_____

DAY 18

Imagine they walk beside you throughout today. What would change?

L ive as if they're near — and they will be. Act as if the veil is already thin.

_____

_____
_____
_____
_____
_____
_____
_____
_____
_____
_____
_____
_____
_____
_____
_____
_____
_____
_____

DAY 19

Choose an object that can represent them—jewelry, stone, keychain. Keep it near as long as you like.

L et it be a tangible symbol. A reminder of the love
you share.

_____
_____
_____
_____
_____
_____
_____
_____
_____
_____
_____
_____
_____
_____

DAY 20

Does narrating your day aloud, as if your loved one is with you, feel good?

L et them in on the little things — your plans, your choices, even your coffee order. Spirit cherishes inclusion, not ceremony. Speak to them as you live your day.

_____

_____

_____

_____

_____

_____

_____

_____

_____

_____

_____

_____

_____

_____

DAY 21

*Have you ever felt their humor or
personality show up again?
What happened?*

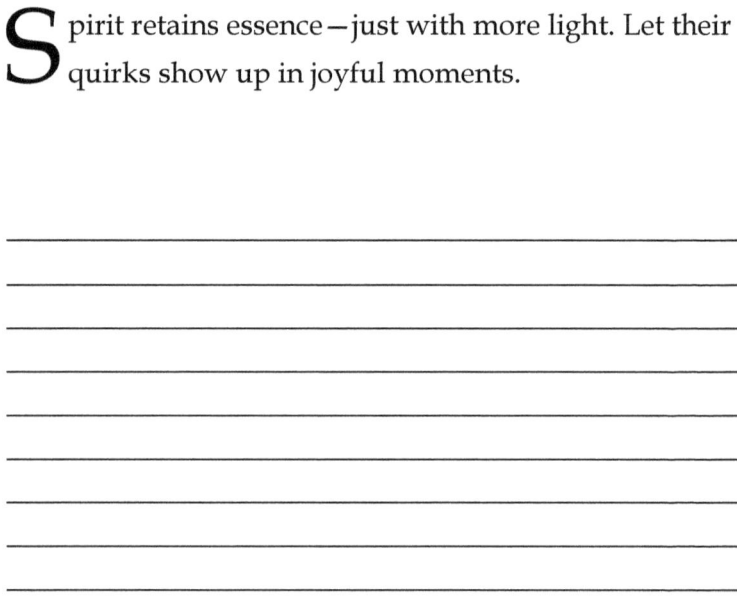

S pirit retains essence — just with more light. Let their
quirks show up in joyful moments.

_____
_____
_____
_____
_____
_____
_____
_____
_____
_____
_____
_____
_____
_____
_____
_____

DAY 22

If you haven't experimented with this, create a small space in your home for them—a photo, candle, token. What does it feel like to visit it?

Y ou're building a sanctuary. This space becomes a sacred pause in your day.

DAY 23

If they could help you through one challenge right now, what would you ask them for?

A sk clearly. Then stay soft and open. Their answer may arrive in subtle form.

_____

_____

_____

_____

_____

_____

_____

_____

_____

_____

_____

_____

_____

_____

_____

DAY 24

What is one thing you do because of them, even now?

T hese habits, gestures, and phrases—they carry energy. Let that continue with love, as long as it flows.

_____

_____

_____

_____

_____

_____

_____

_____

_____

_____

_____

_____

_____

_____

_____

_____

DAY 25

Open a book at random and read the first sentence your eyes land on.

W hat if that line was a message from them, spoken through the page? Spirit often slips between the lines — just enough for you to notice.

DAY 26

Imagine them encouraging you through something mundane but meaningful. What do they say?

Their voice may rise in your mind. Let yourself be cheered on from beyond.

_____

_____

_____

_____

_____

_____

_____

_____

_____

_____

_____

_____

_____

_____

DAY 27

*Place your hand on your heart and ask,
"What are you noticing with me today?"*

L et their presence attune you to the subtle — a
sound, a breeze, a scent. Living with Spirit means
noticing twice, once with your eyes, and once with your
soul.

_____

_____

_____

_____

_____

_____

_____

_____

_____

_____

_____

_____

_____

_____

_____

DAY 28

Write a list titled: "How You Still Walk With Me." Include even the smallest details.

T his becomes a mirror of love's continuity. Every detail is an acknowledgment of your relationship.

_____

_____

_____

_____

_____

_____

_____

_____

_____

_____

_____

_____

_____

_____

_____

_____

_____

_____

DAY 29

*Tell them "Thank you" today—for their
love, their presence, their quiet guidance.*

Gratitude is a bridge. Let it carry your voice to theirs. It honors your connection—still present, still real, still alive in you.

_____
_____
_____
_____
_____
_____
_____
_____
_____
_____
_____
_____
_____
_____
_____
_____

DAY 30

You don't need a special occasion to feel them. They're with you now, and I am too. What everyday moment can you share together today?

This relationship is still alive. Let love meet you right where you are.

_____
_____
_____
_____
_____
_____
_____
_____
_____
_____
_____
_____
_____
_____
_____

MONTH TEN

Rebirth Through Loss

G rief changes you. It dissolves who you were and calls forth someone new — someone deeper, wiser, softer, and stronger all at once. You may not have asked for this transformation, but your soul is rising to meet it.

This month is about honoring the person you're becoming. The grief didn't end your story — it rewrote it. And your loved one in Spirit is still walking beside you as you grow. As a medium, I've witnessed how souls in Spirit are proud of our evolution. They want you to live fully, knowing that your healing is part of their peace too. Let's begin acknowledging your rebirth — together.

DAY 1

How have you changed since your loss—
emotionally, spiritually, or
even physically?

T his evolution is part of your sacred unfolding. Grief
has carved space for your becoming.

_____

_____

_____

_____

_____

_____

_____

_____

_____

_____

_____

_____

_____

_____

DAY 2

What strengths have you discovered in
yourself that you didn't know you had?

G rief awakens what once lay dormant. That strength
is the shape of your soul reclaiming itself.

_____

_____

_____

_____

_____

_____

_____

_____

_____

_____

_____

_____

_____

_____

_____

_____

_____

DAY 3

*Who are you becoming because of this
love—and this loss?*

Y ou are not broken—you are blooming. Let the new
version of you rise with grace.

_____

_____

_____

_____

_____

_____

_____

_____

_____

_____

_____

_____

_____

_____

_____

_____

DAY 4

*If your loved one could describe your soul
right now, what would they say?*

They see you through a lens of unconditional love.
Let their pride become your reflection.

_____

_____

_____

_____

_____

_____

_____

_____

_____

_____

_____

_____

_____

_____

_____

_____

DAY 5

What beliefs or values have shifted in you
since your loss?

G rief reshapes the lens through which you see
everything. Let the shifts reveal not what's
missing, but what's more deeply you now.

_____

_____

_____

_____

_____

_____

_____

_____

_____

_____

_____

_____

_____

_____

_____

DAY 6

What have you let go of since their passing—and what are you learning to hold?

Release and renewal walk hand in hand. Let what no longer serves fall away gently.

_____
_____
_____
_____
_____
_____
_____
_____
_____
_____
_____
_____
_____
_____
_____
_____

DAY 7

Have you become more intuitive, sensitive, or spiritually aware? How does that feel?

T his sensitivity is sacred — not weakness, but awareness. You are attuning to Spirit's frequency.

_____
_____
_____
_____
_____
_____
_____
_____
_____
_____
_____
_____
_____
_____
_____
_____

DAY 8

*If you could create a symbol for who you
are becoming, what would it be?*

This symbol is a mirror of your soul's transformation.
Let it speak what words cannot.

_____

_____

_____

_____

_____

_____

_____

_____

_____

_____

_____

_____

_____

_____

_____

_____

_____

DAY 9

What do you wish the world understood about how grief has changed you?

Y ou are no longer the same—and that's holy. Let the world meet who you've become, not who you were.

_____

_____

_____

_____

_____

_____

_____

_____

_____

_____

_____

_____

_____

_____

_____

DAY 10

What part of your old self do you miss—
and what part do you not want back?

G rieve and bless the parts that faded. Honor the
space now created through growth.

DAY 11

How have your relationships changed? Who do you feel closer to—or further from?

G rief reorders your orbit. Let alignment guide your connections.

_____
_____
_____
_____
_____
_____
_____
_____
_____
_____
_____
_____
_____
_____
_____
_____
_____
_____

DAY 12

What's one thing you've done (big or small)
that would make your loved one proud?

L et their joy echo through your accomplishment.
They are cheering you on.

_____

_____

_____

_____

_____

_____

_____

_____

_____

_____

_____

_____

_____

_____

_____

_____

_____

DAY 13

*Write a "thank you" to the version of you
that survived the early days of loss.*

Y ou held the weight of the unimaginable. Now you
are rising. Let that be honored.

_____

_____

_____

_____

_____

_____

_____

_____

_____

_____

_____

_____

_____

_____

_____

_____

DAY 14

Is there something creative, expressive, or meaningful you've been drawn to since your loss?

✦

Spirit often inspires through creativity. This is co-creation across the veil.

_____

_____

_____

_____

_____

_____

_____

_____

_____

_____

_____

_____

_____

_____

_____

_____

DAY 15

What parts of your life feel like they're being reborn right now?

T his is emergence. Let the new take root without
urgency or pressure.

_____

_____

_____

_____

_____

_____

_____

_____

_____

_____

_____

_____

_____

_____

_____

_____

DAY 16

What boundaries or choices have you made since loss that reflect your growth?

Your clarity is sacred. Let your "no" be as holy as your "yes."

_____

_____

_____

_____

_____

_____

_____

_____

_____

_____

_____

_____

_____

_____

_____

_____

_____

_____

_____

_____

DAY 17

If you could speak to the "you" from a year ago, what wisdom would you share?

B e gentle with the one who didn't know yet. And grateful for the one who kept going.

_____

_____

_____

_____

_____

_____

_____

_____

_____

_____

_____

_____

_____

_____

_____

_____

DAY 18

What role does your loved one still play in your story, even as you evolve?

They are still with you, woven through your choices. The story continues — just in a new chapter.

_____
_____
_____
_____
_____
_____
_____
_____
_____
_____
_____
_____
_____
_____
_____
_____

DAY 19

Write a mantra or affirmation that speaks to the soul you're becoming.

Maybe it's something like: "I am stronger now" or "I am present with my heart". Make it your declaration of becoming.

DAY 20

Do you feel like a different person than before they passed? In what ways?

Change is not disloyalty — it's a sign of life. Honor the difference as a doorway.

_____

_____

_____

_____

_____

_____

_____

_____

_____

_____

_____

_____

_____

_____

_____

_____

DAY 21

How would you describe your current relationship with grief? Is it shifting? Softening? Deepening?

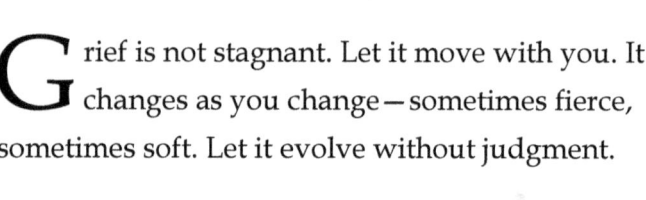

G rief is not stagnant. Let it move with you. It changes as you change—sometimes fierce, sometimes soft. Let it evolve without judgment.

_____
_____
_____
_____
_____
_____
_____
_____
_____
_____
_____
_____
_____
_____

DAY 22

What dreams or desires are returning to you now, after a long pause?

S pirit may be gently nudging you into a new version of life. Receive what's returning and open to what's being created.

_____
_____
_____
_____
_____
_____
_____
_____
_____
_____
_____
_____
_____
_____
_____

DAY 23

What does "healing" mean to you now?
Has that definition changed?

Healing is no longer a destination — it's a natural journey. Let it walk beside you and within you.

_____
_____
_____
_____
_____
_____
_____
_____
_____
_____
_____
_____
_____
_____
_____
_____

DAY 24

What's one new part of your identity you've embraced since loss?

Y ou are integrating, not erasing. Let this new version of you be seen, without apology.

DAY 25

If your loved one could give you permission to step into something new, what would it be?

T hey want you to live. Fully. Freely. Joyfully. Let their blessing be felt deeply.

DAY 26

How has your capacity for love deepened
since they passed?

✦

Grief stretches the heart in ever-expanding ways.
You are loving with more depth than ever before.

_____

_____

_____

_____

_____

_____

_____

_____

_____

_____

_____

_____

_____

_____

_____

_____

_____

_____

DAY 27

Create a vision for the next chapter of your life. How is your loved one contributing to it?

Y ou bring the gifts of your love and experience into what comes next. Let the future be shaped by the imprint they've left on your heart.

_____
_____
_____
_____
_____
_____
_____
_____
_____
_____
_____
_____
_____
_____

DAY 28

What part of their essence lives on through the way you love, choose, and create?

Y our life becomes a living tribute, not in burden — but in quiet reverence. Even the simplest act, done with presence, becomes a sacred offering.

_____
_____
_____
_____
_____
_____
_____
_____
_____
_____
_____
_____
_____
_____
_____
_____
_____

DAY 29

Name something you once feared that
now feels less scary. What shifted?

✦

G rief transformed your relationship with fear. Let
your steady heart show you the way.

_____

_____

_____

_____

_____

_____

_____

_____

_____

_____

_____

_____

_____

_____

_____

_____

DAY 30

You are rising. Your loved one sees you.
What part of yourself are you
ready to claim?

This is your rebirth. Sacred. Real. Beautiful. Let your light rise from the roots of your love.

_____
_____
_____
_____
_____
_____
_____
_____
_____
_____
_____
_____
_____
_____
_____
_____

MONTH ELEVEN

Living with Presence

G rief doesn't disappear — but it softens. And as it softens, space begins to open. More space for breath. For beauty. For moments of joy that don't erase the pain, but sit beside it.

This month is about learning to live again — with presence, with gratitude, and with your loved one still close, even in their new form. I know that Spirit celebrates when we return to life. Your loved one doesn't want you to feel guilty for smiling, for laughing, for healing. They're walking with you as you rediscover how to live — not just survive.

DAY 1

What small thing brought you peace or beauty today? Describe it with presence.

S pirit often sends comfort through life's quietest details. This is where you allow yourself to sense their love gently — through noticing.

_____

_____

_____

_____

_____

_____

_____

_____

_____

_____

_____

_____

_____

_____

_____

_____

_____

DAY 2

*What does joy feel like in your body?
When did you last feel it, even for
a moment?*

J oy is not a betrayal—it is a remembering. Let your joy become an aspect of welcoming the new chapter of life.

_____

_____

_____

_____

_____

_____

_____

_____

_____

_____

_____

_____

_____

_____

_____

_____

_____

DAY 3

Write about a moment when you felt fully alive since your loss. What were you doing?

T hat aliveness is sacred. It means your soul is healing. Even small moments of joy are signs of resilience — honor them without guilt.

DAY 4

What daily ritual helps you stay grounded? Can you bring more presence to it?

The ordinary becomes sacred when witnessed with presence. Spirit often meets you in the quiet ritual.

_____

_____

_____

_____

_____

_____

_____

_____

_____

_____

_____

_____

_____

_____

_____

DAY 5

*Describe your surroundings right now
using all five senses. What do you notice?*

Your senses are sacred messengers. Let them draw
you back into the brightness of the world.

_____
_____
_____
_____
_____
_____
_____
_____
_____
_____
_____
_____
_____
_____
_____
_____

DAY 6

What's one part of your day where you tend to "check out"? Can you open up there?

That overlooked moment might be quietly asking for your presence. Let your noticing become a doorway to something deeper.

_____
_____
_____
_____
_____
_____
_____
_____
_____
_____
_____
_____
_____
_____

DAY 7

Write about a time laughter surprised you in your grief. Did it soothe something in you?

L aughter does not erase love — it extends it. Let joy cleanse your sorrow gently.

_____
_____
_____
_____
_____
_____
_____
_____
_____
_____
_____
_____
_____
_____
_____
_____

DAY 8

What's one thing your loved one appreciated or enjoyed, that you can remember today?

L et this remembrance become a communion. You are keeping their joy alive through your acknowledgment.

_____
_____
_____
_____
_____
_____
_____
_____
_____
_____
_____
_____
_____
_____
_____
_____

DAY 9

*Name three things you're grateful for
today, even in the midst of pain.*

G ratitude holds the door open to presence. It reminds you that beauty still exists.

_____
_____
_____
_____
_____
_____
_____
_____
_____
_____
_____
_____
_____
_____
_____
_____
_____

DAY 10

*If your loved one could spend this day
with you in the physical, what would you
do together?*

✦

L et this vision guide how you live today. Spirit joins
you in these moments.

_____

_____

_____

_____

_____

_____

_____

_____

_____

_____

_____

_____

_____

_____

_____

_____

_____

DAY 11

Write a prayer, poem, or message of appreciation to the moment you're in right now.

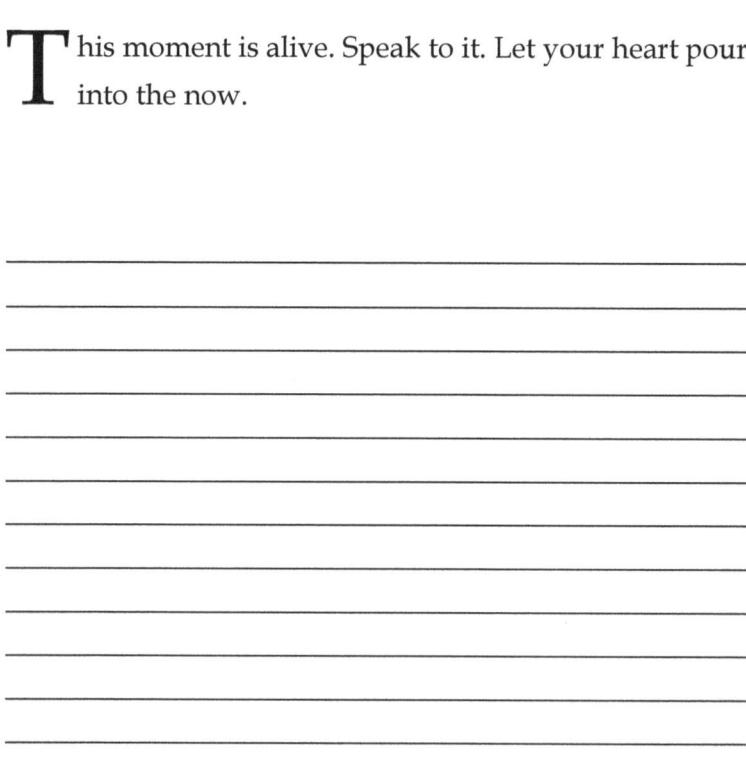

This moment is alive. Speak to it. Let your heart pour into the now.

_____

_____

_____

_____

_____

_____

_____

_____

_____

_____

_____

_____

_____

_____

_____

DAY 12

What colors, textures, or images feel comforting to you lately? Surround yourself with them.

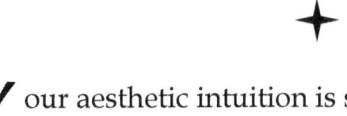

Your aesthetic intuition is sacred. Let your environment echo your soul.

_____

_____

_____

_____

_____

_____

_____

_____

_____

_____

_____

_____

_____

_____

_____

_____

_____

_____

DAY 13

What does self-care look like today, to the
version of you who is grieving and growing?

✦

This self is worthy of tending. Let your care be slow, intentional, and full of grace.

_____

_____

_____

_____

_____

_____

_____

_____

_____

_____

_____

_____

_____

_____

_____

DAY 14

What time of day do you feel the most connected to life? Why do you think that is?

There may be a window there — an opening to Spirit. Honor that sacred rhythm.

DAY 15

Write about a meal, a walk, or a moment of silence that brought clarity.

✦

Stillness can become sanctuary. Let that clarity be your gentle guide.

_____

_____

_____

_____

_____

_____

_____

_____

_____

_____

_____

_____

_____

_____

_____

_____

_____

DAY 16

What's one thing you've seen recently that
reminded you that life is still beautiful?

E ven the smallest beauty is a bridge to life. Let it fill
you, even if only for a moment.

_____

_____

_____

_____

_____

_____

_____

_____

_____

_____

_____

_____

_____

_____

DAY 17

Have you experienced a moment of grace in your grief? Describe it.

✦

Grace is Spirit's way of saying: "You're not alone." Let that moment wrap around you again.

_____

_____

_____

_____

_____

_____

_____

_____

_____

_____

_____

_____

_____

_____

_____

_____

DAY 18

Create a short affirmation that brings you back to the present. Repeat it today.

Presence opens the portal to peace. Let this affirmation become your anchor.

_____
_____
_____
_____
_____
_____
_____
_____
_____
_____
_____
_____
_____
_____
_____
_____

DAY 19

When you feel yourself rushing or disconnecting, what can bring you back?

✦

One breath. One pause. One remembering. Let your breath become your bridge to the present.

_____

_____

_____

_____

_____

_____

_____

_____

_____

_____

_____

_____

_____

_____

_____

_____

DAY 20

Write a thank-you letter to the day.
What did it offer, even quietly?

E very day offers something sacred. Let today reveal
its quiet gifts.

_____

_____

_____

_____

_____

_____

_____

_____

_____

_____

_____

_____

_____

_____

_____

_____

DAY 21

What simple pleasure could you allow yourself without guilt today?

✦

Your joy is part of your healing. You are allowed to receive.

_____
_____
_____
_____
_____
_____
_____
_____
_____
_____
_____
_____
_____
_____
_____
_____
_____

DAY 22

How would it feel to live with grief, rather than against it? Describe that possibility.

✦

Grief can walk beside joy. Often they both become companions on the path.

DAY 23

Name one way your loved one's presence lives on in your everyday life.

You carry their essence through your being. Let that be enough.

_____
_____
_____
_____
_____
_____
_____
_____
_____
_____
_____
_____
_____
_____
_____
_____
_____

DAY 24

Create a "moment of presence" practice:
choose one time a day to pause
and check in.

S pirit often enters through the quiet we allow. This
pause becomes a place of gentle reunion.

DAY 25

When you slow down, what part of you feels most alive? Most tender? Most open?

✦

S lowness reveals what is most real. Let yourself be witnessed in this way.

_____

_____

_____

_____

_____

_____

_____

_____

_____

_____

_____

_____

_____

_____

_____

DAY 26

If you could ask this moment a question,
what would it be? What might it say back?

The present moment holds its own wisdom. Listen
gently — it may speak through feeling.

DAY 27

Write about how your relationship to time has changed since your loss.

S pirit's rhythm is not linear. You're learning to live by soul-time now.

_____

_____

_____

_____

_____

_____

_____

_____

_____

_____

_____

_____

_____

_____

_____

DAY 28

*What would it mean to live today as a
sacred experience, even in its ordinariness?*

L et the ordinary reveal its hidden holiness. This is
where Spirit softly gathers.

_____

_____

_____

_____

_____

_____

_____

_____

_____

_____

_____

_____

_____

_____

_____

_____

_____

DAY 29

Imagine your loved one smiling at you right now. What do they want you to notice or enjoy today?

L et their smile soak in. Receive this moment as a gift. Breathe into this moment. Let your body remember what it feels like to be here.

_____

_____

_____

_____

_____

_____

_____

_____

_____

_____

_____

_____

_____

_____

DAY 30

You're allowed to be present. To feel peace. To heal. And I'm right here with you as you do. What's one thing you'll do today to honor your beautiful, loving heart?

This is your return to new life. Let your healing heart lead you home.

_____
_____
_____
_____
_____
_____
_____
_____
_____
_____
_____
_____
_____
_____
_____

MONTH TWELVE

The Love That Remains

You've walked through the ache of absence, the mystery of Spirit, the weight of memory, and the beauty of healing. And now, here you are — still grieving, still growing, still loving.

This month is not about closure. It's about integration. About recognizing that love never ends — it only changes form. Your loved one is not behind you. They are beside you, within you, and all around you. As a psychic medium, I've seen the truth of this over and over again: the love remains. Let this final chapter be a celebration of that sacred, ongoing connection.

DAY 1

What does your love for them feel like today? How has it transformed over time?

L ove doesn't vanish — it deepens. Let the love you feel today be your sacred knowing.

_____

_____
_____
_____
_____
_____
_____
_____
_____
_____
_____
_____
_____
_____
_____
_____
_____
_____
_____

DAY 2

What would you say if you could thank them for the love they gave you?

✦

Speak it now. They are listening. Your words travel across realms.

_____
_____
_____
_____
_____
_____
_____
_____
_____
_____
_____
_____
_____
_____
_____
_____
_____
_____

DAY 3

*If your grief could speak to your love,
what would it say?*

✦

Grief is love's shadow. Let them speak to each other with truth.

_____
_____
_____
_____
_____
_____
_____
_____
_____
_____
_____
_____
_____
_____
_____
_____
_____

DAY 4

Name three ways they still live on through you.

They echo through the way you love, speak, and simply are. They move through your choices, your compassion, your light.

_____
_____
_____
_____
_____
_____
_____
_____
_____
_____
_____
_____
_____
_____
_____
_____
_____

DAY 5

How do you carry their essence into the world now?

Their presence and their absence has changed you. Let what's come through their presence flow through your being.

_____

_____

_____

_____

_____

_____

_____

_____

_____

_____

_____

_____

_____

_____

_____

_____

DAY 6

*What have they taught you about life,
death, and what truly matters?*

Their passing opened a door to soul-level healing.
Let that clarity shape your next steps.

_____

_____

_____

_____

_____

_____

_____

_____

_____

_____

_____

_____

_____

_____

_____

_____

_____

DAY 7

Write about the love you feel with them now—not just for them.

T his is not just memory — it is relationship. Let the connection remain alive.

_____

_____
_____
_____
_____
_____
_____
_____
_____
_____
_____
_____
_____
_____
_____
_____
_____

DAY 8

What does "forever" mean to you, now that they're in Spirit?

Forever is not time — it is truth. Let it live in presence, not distance.

_____

_____

_____

_____

_____

_____

_____

_____

_____

_____

_____

_____

_____

_____

_____

_____

_____

_____

DAY 9

Describe what it feels like when you know they're near. What does that presence offer you?

Their nearness may arrive in peace, warmth, or sudden knowing. Let that feeling soothe your soul.

_____

_____

_____

_____

_____

_____

_____

_____

_____

_____

_____

_____

_____

DAY 10

Write a love letter from your soul to theirs. Let it be soft, honest, and whole.

L et your heart speak freely. This is your soul speaking directly to theirs.

_____
_____
_____
_____
_____
_____
_____
_____
_____
_____
_____
_____
_____
_____
_____
_____
_____
_____

DAY 11

If you could carry one final message from them into the next chapter of your life, what would it be?

This message is already echoing within you. It waits to be spoken through the way you live, the way you love.

_____
_____
_____
_____
_____
_____
_____
_____
_____
_____
_____
_____
_____
_____

DAY 12

What would it mean to live the rest of your life as an act of love—for them, for yourself, for life itself?

T his is what they hold for you. Let your life become a radiant expression.

_____

_____

_____

_____

_____

_____

_____

_____

_____

_____

_____

_____

_____

_____

_____

DAY 13

*Name something you once feared would
fade that has, in fact, endured.*

W hat lasts reveals the truth of love. Let that truth
steady you as you walk forward.

_____
_____
_____
_____
_____
_____
_____
_____
_____
_____
_____
_____
_____
_____
_____
_____
_____
_____
_____

DAY 14

*What does your connection feel like now,
compared to the beginning of your grief?*

Y ou've built a new chapter. Let that evolution be
your soul's quiet testament to love.

_____
_____
_____
_____
_____
_____
_____
_____
_____
_____
_____
_____
_____
_____
_____
_____
_____
_____

DAY 15

What's one memory you return to over and over again? Does it support you?

I f it's supportive, let that memory be their gift to you — still living. Let it nourish your soul again and again. If it's not, is it time to release it?

_____

_____

_____

_____

_____

_____

_____

_____

_____

_____

_____

_____

_____

_____

_____

_____

DAY 16

Write about a "full circle" moment—
something that healed or completed
itself unexpectedly.

T hese sacred loops are Spirit's way of affirming: all is
held. Let it remind you of the grace that found you.

_____
_____
_____
_____
_____
_____
_____
_____
_____
_____
_____
_____
_____
_____
_____
_____
_____

DAY 17

What would it feel like to let yourself live fully while also holding them in your heart?

It's not one or the other. Let joy and remembrance coexist. Your love makes room for both.

_____
_____
_____
_____
_____
_____
_____
_____
_____
_____
_____
_____
_____
_____
_____
_____

DAY 18

Do you feel them cheering you on from Spirit? What might they be celebrating today?

T hey see your becoming. Let yourself feel their pride. You are growing in ways they would cherish. Let their love echo in your courage.

_____

_____

_____

_____

_____

_____

_____

_____

_____

_____

_____

_____

_____

_____

_____

DAY 19

Create a list titled: "This is the Love That Remains." Include memories, lessons, gestures, symbols.

This is your altar of remembrance. Return to it when you forget.

_____

_____

_____

_____

_____

_____

_____

_____

_____

_____

_____

_____

_____

_____

_____

_____

_____

DAY 20

What would you want to tell someone who's just beginning their grief journey?

L et your lived experience offer comfort. Your voice may become someone else's lighthouse.

_____
_____
_____
_____
_____
_____
_____
_____
_____
_____
_____
_____
_____
_____
_____
_____
_____

DAY 21

How will you honor their memory moving forward—not just in sorrow, but in celebration?

Honor can be joyful. Let their memory inspire your light. Carry them not just in tears, but in the beauty you continue to create.

DAY 22

What does your soul feel ready for, now that so much has been released?

Y ou are making space for joy, purpose, and renewal. Let yourself receive what's next.

_____

_____

_____

_____

_____

_____

_____

_____

_____

_____

_____

_____

_____

_____

_____

_____

_____

_____

DAY 23

Imagine your loved one placing their hand
on your heart. What do you feel?

T hat warmth is more than comfort—it's confirmation.
Let it remind you: you are never alone.

_____
_____
_____
_____
_____
_____
_____
_____
_____
_____
_____
_____
_____
_____
_____
_____
_____

DAY 24

What part of you is more open, more loving,
or more present because of this grief?

Your expansion is sacred. That tenderness has
developed your strength.

_____
_____
_____
_____
_____
_____
_____
_____
_____
_____
_____
_____
_____
_____
_____
_____

DAY 25

Name a dream or hope you have. How can their energy support you in reaching it?

Y ou're co-creating with them now. Let them walk beside your dream.

_____
_____
_____
_____
_____
_____
_____
_____
_____
_____
_____
_____
_____
_____
_____

DAY 26

What does the phrase "they're with me"
mean to you now?

I t's more than metaphor—it's your lived truth. They
are woven into your now.

DAY 27

Write a message from your future self—who has continued to heal, grow, and live fully. What do they want you to know?

That version of you carries love lightly and deeply. Let their words lift you higher and higher.

DAY 28

What does "peace" feel like today? Is there more of it in you now?

P eace is presence with what is. Let it settle in as softly as a feather falling to the earth.

_____

_____

_____

_____

_____

_____

_____

_____

_____

_____

_____

_____

_____

_____

_____

_____

_____

DAY 29

In what ways have you surprised yourself during this journey? What strengths have you uncovered?

Y ou are wiser than you were before, and braver than your fear. What once may have felt like it broke you, now sings through you.

_____
_____
_____
_____
_____
_____
_____
_____
_____
_____
_____
_____
_____
_____
_____
_____

DAY 30

Love has never left you. And neither have they. What will you carry forward from this year—this sacred walk through grief, love, and Spirit?

This is your sacred threshold—both closure and emergence. A soul-bond eternal, unfolding beyond form.

_____

_____

_____

_____

_____

_____

_____

_____

_____

_____

_____

_____

_____

_____

_____

Let the love that remains illuminate your way.

Acknowledgements

To the ones I've loved and lost—thank you for showing me that absence can become a doorway, and that grief, when honored, becomes a sacred teacher. You continue to guide me in ways I never expected.

To my clients, students, and grieving hearts who have shared your most tender truths with me—your courage has shaped every page of this book. Thank you for sharing your healing path with me.

To my Spirit collaborators, the luminous souls beyond the veil, and the divine rhythm that moves through it all—thank you for whispering the words, holding the field, and reminding us: love does not end. It evolves.

And to you, beloved reader—thank you for saying yes to the path of feeling,

for letting love lead you, and for trusting this companion as you stay connected to the one you love—and to the you that you're meeting, moment by moment, as you walk this path.